SABOTAGE

SABOTAGE

THE HIDDEN NATURE
OF FINANCE

—

**ANASTASIA NESVETAILOVA
AND RONEN PALAN**

PUBLICAFFAIRS

New York

PublicAffairs

Hachette Book Group

1290 Avenue of the Americas, New York, NY 10104

www.publicaffairsbooks.com

@Public_Affairs

Printed in the United States of America

First Edition: January 2020

Published by PublicAffairs, an imprint of Perseus Books, LLC, a subsidiary of Hachette Book Group, Inc. The PublicAffairs name and logo is a trademark of the Hachette Book Group.

The Hachette Speakers Bureau provides a wide range of authors for speaking events. To find out more, go to www.hachettespeakersbureau.com or call (866) 376-6591.

The publisher is not responsible for websites (or their content) that are not owned by the publisher.

Library of Congress Cataloging-in-Publication Data

Names: Nesvetailova, Anastasia, author. | Palan, Ronen, 1957– author.

Title: Sabotage: the hidden nature of finance / Anastasia Nesvetailova, Ronen Palan.

Description: First edition. | New York: PublicAffairs, [2019] | Includes bibliographical references and index.

Identifiers: LCCN 2019033094 | ISBN 9781610399685 (hardcover) | ISBN 9781610399692 (ebook)

Subjects: LCSH: United States—Economic policy. | Monetary policy—United States—History. | Finance—United States—History. | Recessions—United States—History. | Financial crises—United States—History.

Classification: LCC HC103 .N45 2019 | DDC 332.0973—dc23

LC record available at https://lccn.loc.gov/2019033094

ISBNs: 978-1-61039-968-5 (hardcover), 978-1-61039-969-2 (ebook)

LSC-C

10 9 8 7 6 5 4 3 2 1

To Michael and Sasha

CONTENTS

Contents

ABBREVIATIONS AND TERMS

AIG: American Insurance Group.

CDO: Collateralized default obligations.

CDS: Credit default swap. A financial contract whereby a buyer of corporate or sovereign debt in the form of bonds attempts to eliminate possible loss arising from default by the issuer of the bonds. This is achieved by the issuer of the bonds insuring the buyer's potential losses as part of the agreement.

EMT: Efficient market theory.

EPAs: Equity participation agreements. A type of contract.

Glass–Steagall Act (1933): A major legislative piece of the regulatory foundations of the post-1929 economy in the US. Sponsored in Congress by Senator Carter Glass and Representative Carter Steagall, the Glass–Steagall Act separated commercial and investment banking functions in the financial system of the US. It was repealed in 1999.

GRG: Global Restructuring Group. GRG was the former turnaround division of RBS/NatWest. Many business banking customers of RBS and NatWest were informed they were over-geared or underperforming, and as such were transferred to the unit. After the onset of the financial crisis, 16,000 companies were allegedly pushed into GRG (https://senecabanking.co.uk/global-restructuring-group/).

ICO (ITO): Initial coin offering (initial token offering). In an ICO, a quantity of cryptocurrency is sold in the form of 'tokens' ('coins') to speculators or investors in exchange for legal tender or other cryptocurrencies. The tokens sold are promoted as future functional units of currency if or when the ICO's funding goal is met and the project launches.

LIBOR: London interbank offered rate. A benchmark rate at which major global banks lend to one another in the international interbank market for short-term loans.

'London Whale': The nickname of a trader, Bruno Iksil, who lost at least $6.2bn for J. P. Morgan Chase & Co. in 2012.

MBS: Mortgage-backed securities. A financial instrument similar to a bond. It is created out of a bundle of home loans bought from the banks that issued them. Investors in MBS receive periodic payments similar to bond coupon payments.

OIE: Old institutional economics.

OPM: Other people's money.

PPFAs: Property participation fee agreements. A type of contract which provides for a return or payment from the bank's customer, and which is linked to the value of the customer's asset(s).

Risk-weighted assets: A criterion used to determine the minimum amount of capital that must be held by banks and other institutions to reduce the risk of insolvency.

RMBS: Residential mortgage-backed securities.

SEC: Securities and Exchange Commission (USA).

TBTF: Too big to fail.

INTRODUCTION

EVERYONE WANTS TO BE
LIKE GOLDMAN

In June 2016, in the wake of the fallen Gaddafi regime, the Libyan authorities sued Goldman Sachs for nine trades the bank advised on and then executed for the Libyan sovereign wealth fund between January and April 2008. The new Libyan government claimed that Goldman Sachs gained more than $200m in profits from the trade, whereas the Libyans lost almost all their investment.

It would transpire during court proceedings that Goldman paid for prostitutes, private jets and five-star hotels to win the business from a Libyan investment fund. Goldman's internal documents describe its Libyan clients as having 'zero-level' of financial sophistication. The bank's documents advised that 'it is important you stay super close to clients on a daily basis.' One Goldman Sachs employee describes how he 'delivered a pitch on structured leveraged loans to someone who lives in the middle of the desert with his camels'.[1]

Libya lost the case. In October 2016 a High Court judge in London found that the relationship between Goldman Sachs and the Libyan Investment Authority 'did not go beyond the normal cordial and mutually beneficial relationship that grows up between a bank and a client'. In the judge's opinion Goldman's fees in the disputed trades were not excessive given 'the nature of the trades and the work that had gone into winning them'.[2]

In finance everyone wants to be like Goldman. Having started in 1869 as a small brokerage firm, the company changed its name to Goldman Sachs in 1882. By the early twentieth century the firm had grown to become one of the greatest of American institutions, associated perhaps more than any other company with American power and financial prowess. Goldman continually tops the list of dream jobs for graduates; Goldman's alumni are among the highest-profile policymakers around the world. Throughout its history, the company has shown an extraordinary ability to adapt and to anticipate change.

'What makes Goldman Sachs so special?' asks Lisa Endlich in her bestselling book, *Goldman Sachs: The Culture of Success*. Endlich's answer reads like many of the hagiographies produced along the years: Goldman's success has to do with its 'unique culture', the culture of hard work. 'You must be able to give away many other things in your life if you are willing to succeed at GS. It's more like a lifestyle and a whole life career than just a job.'[3]

In 2010 the US Securities and Exchange Commission (SEC) came up with a slightly different description of the 'culture' of Goldman. The SEC charged Goldman and one of its vice presidents (VPs) with defrauding investors by 'misstating and omitting key facts about a financial product'.[4] The SEC alleged that Goldman Sachs had selected securities for their customers without disclosing an important piece of information. Specifically, that a hedge fund closely associated with Goldman, Paulson & Co., participated in the selection of the portfolio to be sold to clients, only to bet against it. In other words Goldman sold its customers securities it believed were going to fail. In the process Goldman gained twice, while its customers lost twice: Goldman Sachs charged commission on brokerage and an advice fee, whereas the customers ended up paying not only the fees but also the losses on a bet Goldman advised them to take. This affair became known as the 'Abacus deal'.[5] We discuss it in detail in Chapter 5.

Was Abacus an isolated case? Not so, argues a former Goldman executive. He summed up his career advice to ambitious young entrants to the firm in three golden principles:

1) Execute on the firm's 'axes', which is 'Goldman-speak' for persuading your clients to invest in the stocks or other products that we are trying to get rid of because they are not seen as having a lot of potential profit.
2) 'Hunt Elephants.' In plain English: get your clients – some of whom are sophisticated and some aren't – to trade whatever will bring the biggest profit to Goldman.
3) Find yourself sitting in a seat where your job is to trade any illiquid, opaque product with a three-letter acronym.[6]

So who is right, then? Is it Lisa Endlich's celebratory study of Goldman's culture, or the former executive describing a culture of short-termism and cynicism, combined with extraordinary ruthlessness?

We think that both are right. In finance people tend to work hard, very hard. They also tend to be among the smartest around. They have to be: the system in which they operate is fast-changing, competitive and very, very tough. But working hard or being smart is not good enough in today's financial markets. Finance is a fiercely dynamic and competitive industry, with capital markets being among the closest to what academics call the 'efficient market hypothesis (EMH)'.

Proposed by, among others, two Nobel laureates, Paul Samuelson and Eugene Fama, EMH is often misunderstood. It tends to be simplified to imply that 'markets know best'. The theory appears to suggest that markets allocate resources so efficiently and quickly that no outside intervention by governments or regulators is ever needed. EMH can be, and has been, easily ridiculed any time the market fails, as, for instance, during a financial crisis.

But this is not the most important interpretation of EMH, or even, in our view, a correct one. The idea of market efficiency has a deeper and a more sobering implication: namely, that however clever you might be, and however hard you might work, you can never beat the market. There is no way, EMH tells us, that anyone can make profits consistently over time just trading by the rules of the market. EHM prompts us to move away from the idea that financial and banking institutions have superior skills at reading economic data and financial trends and are able to understand the future better than anyone else. As Paul Samuelson wrote: 'Perhaps there really are managers who can outperform the market consistently – logic would suggest that they exist. But they are remarkably well hidden.'[7]

In finance there seems to be a unique concentration of very smart people who work very hard to make money, and very often succeed. Before 2007, profits of 20–30 per cent, even over 40 per cent, of turnover were not unheard of in finance. After 2009, profits are still very high. Yet according to the theory there should not be such profits in finance. Even if we make adjustments to market-augmenting factors such as barriers to entry (to exist, banks need licences), regulatory interference (rules such as the Basel accord) and other barriers (differences in currency regimes, accounting rules, controls over capital flows, etc.), there is little in the structure of the deep, liquid and globalized markets for capital that can explain the level of superprofits the industry had become accustomed to.

So what is the source of those superprofits? Where do they come from, then? Did theoreticians get it wrong? Should we strip Samuelson and Fama of their Nobel Prizes? Perhaps not. There is, in fact, a way of making good money in finance, and it is not new. To learn about it, we just have to listen a bit more carefully to those who work the engine rooms of finance, the CEOs and those inhabiting the trading floors. They seem to have a pretty good idea of how to deal with the constraints of efficient markets.

An anecdote is making the rounds in financial circles. A few weeks prior to its collapse, executives at Lehman Brothers are said to have gathered for a meeting to plan investment decisions. When a particular deal was discussed, one of the directors raised a query about a potential conflict of interest in the case. The chair of the meeting reportedly retorted: 'no conflict, no interest.'

One might think that Lehman is an exception: a bank that had got carried away in the hype of easy money and eventually succumbed to its own negligence and incompetence. But Lehman is not an aberration. The 'no conflict, no interest' mantra captures, as we will see in this book, a much wider phenomenon than the failings of an individual bank. It captures the mode of behaviour, the thinking, the zeitgeist, that has become standard in the industry.

We do not need to venture far to find evidence for such behaviour. A UK parliamentary committee concluded that two of the bailed-out British banks, RBS and Lloyds, 'deliberately and systematically' pushed their clients among the small- and medium-sized companies into default. Why? In order to seize their assets 'on the cheap'. In 2009 UBS, the largest Swiss bank, negotiated a deferred-prosecution agreement with the US Justice Department in a probe of tax evasion. So did Credit Suisse, and a host of other Swiss, Israeli and Indian banks. HSBC was charged with (and admitted to) failing to monitor more than $670bn in wire transfers and more than $9.4bn in purchases of US currency from HSBC Mexico. One of the premier world banks in the world admitted to facilitating money laundering for the Mexican drug cartels! HSBC joined BNP Paribas and other banks in violating US economic sanctions against Iran, Libya, Sudan, Burma and Cuba. A separate US investigation into how banks helped and abetted tax evasion brought down Wegelin, the oldest Swiss bank, which closed its doors in 2013 after 272 years in business. The bank's final act was to plead guilty to US charges of tax fraud.[8]

On this side of the Atlantic, the LIBOR affair broke out in 2012, closely followed by Euribor and the foreign exchange rigging cases, as well as a myriad of cases of 'mis-selling'. In 2015 Deutsche Bank – whose presence in Russia dates back to 1881 – had to shut its Russian securities unit under three US investigations into the bank's role in helping Russian clients launder funds and take money out of the country in so-called mirror deals, totalling $6bn.[9] In 2018 Danske Bank, Denmark's largest banking institution and one of the most respected in Europe, was revealed to have been involved in a money-laundering scheme via its Estonian subsidiary, to the tune of some $234bn. As this book goes to press, Nordea, another respected Scandinavian bank, is facing similar allegations of enabling corruption.

Banks' less serious misdeeds include, but are not confined to, the following: misleading statements to investors involving capital-raising rights issues; abusive lending practices to small businesses; manipulation of gold prices; misreporting related to Barclays emergency capital raising; a banker stealing confidential regulatory information; collusion with Greek authorities to mislead EU policymakers on meeting euro criteria; financial engineering with the aim of moving Italian debt off balance sheet; manipulation of risk models with the aim of minimizing reported risk-weighted assets/capital requirements; filing false statements with the SEC and keeping false books and records, or what has become known as the 'London Whale' story.[10] The list is likely to be incomplete by the time this book is published.

Since 2009, American and foreign banks have paid out $321bn in fines for misbehaviour in the US alone. This is a handy sum. It suggests to us that big, international banks are prepared to take great risks with the law. It implies that the theory that such behaviour is produced by rogue elements within banking is incorrect. The malaise is systemic.

But even if, despite the lengthy lists of cases and the hefty fines, one would still wish to describe these episodes as products of the behaviour of rogue elements, it still remains to be explained why rogue elements flourish in finance and, specifically, why they seem to flourish at a particular time and place.

The crisis of 2007–9 is commonly explained as the outcome of poor global macroeconomic policies and inadequate regulatory frameworks. But what is the connection between global macro-policies and banks having lost their moral compass? If these incidences are isolated cases of failed governance, how come the most sophisticated, mobile financial corporations which invest billions in IT to cut down a fraction of time in algorithmic trading, and in controlling asset values that reach trillions of dollars, were so poorly managed that one hand did not know what the other had been doing *for such a long time*? What does failure on such a superlative scale tell us about the culture of finance and, more specifically, the business standard in the industry? Is there even a kernel of hope that such episodes are whittled down to a minimum in the future?

THE BASIC TRUTH ABOUT PROFITABILITY

Our principal contention in this book is that finance needs to be understood first and foremost as a business. It is simple idea. Corporate entities, and the individuals who work for them, at least those in positions of power and decision-making (the proverbial 'dealmakers'), should be viewed above all else as businessmen and businesswomen. As business people, they are not beholden to any particular theory of what banking should be about. They are interested in money, in pecuniary gain.

Big deal, you may think. Everyone knows that banking and finance are about money and profit. But here nuances do matter. It is the theory of *how* business makes money that is important. The conventional conception of a business, including banking, is of a trading entity that is subject to market discipline. Unlike manufacturing firms, which produce something, the theoretical function of financial markets is to connect borrowers and savers.

The more efficiently they do this, the better we all are. Because if trading units operate in competitive markets, then they will be forced to innovate, make efficiency gains and ultimately optimize societal resource allocation. States and governments are encouraged, therefore, to curb their natural tendency to intervene in the markets, including the financial markets.

There are many problems with the theory, and they have been discussed ad nauseam in wider literature. The efficient market hypothesis is only one variant of a core assumption of standard economics. It suggests that in the long run profits in perfectly competitive markets are close to zero. As new firms enter the industry, they increase the supply of the product available in the market, forcing prices down to the point of near-zero profits. Profits, in other words, result from what economists call 'transitory disequilibria' in the market. This is good, economics tells us, because market disequilibria occur through innovation in product, services, delivery or organization; or, alternatively, due to exogenous perturbations such as political interference.

This may indeed be the case, but this theory works provided two assumptions are met. First, it works as long as transitory disequilibria are generated by behaviour that follows certain norms. But what if not everyone plays by the rules? Since the implication of the theory is that those businesses who play by the rules will only be delaying and deferring the inevitable – loss of profit and collapse – while running at very low profitability in the meantime, the question arises whether those businesses may not seek a more permanent solution to their problem, a more permanent 'disequilibrium' in the markets, to ensure that the discipline of the price mechanism may apply to *others*, but less so to them.

Perhaps, and this is our core contention, the business of finance is not that different to other businesses. There is a long tradition of thought and research that shows how successful industrial or services businesses seek ways of interfering with the market, by influencing it, changing it in such a way that competition rules do not apply to them – and, ideally, *exclusively* not to them. Both Coca-Cola and Pepsi are happy to sing songs of praise to the competitive free market while signing exclusive deals with restaurants and venues so that the customers have no choice in the matter. Those deals do not seem to be intended to generate greater efficiency or 'optimal' resource allocations. Nor do restaurants and other venues particularly welcome such deals. These deals aim to ensure higher profitability of these two competitors, by monopolizing outlets. We know that today's high-tech giants – Apple, Amazon, Google, Facebook or Microsoft – will do anything to control competition in their 'markets', by purchasing or destroying potential new entrants.

Why should finance act differently? Why should we think that some of the most perceptive business people around, those at the helm of institutions with colossal market power, would tend to play by the rules that academic theory imagines to be the rules of the market? Like any business, finance faces the challenge of competitive markets: competition is the enemy of profits. That many banking and financial houses are highly profitable only shows us that individually and collectively they have found ways of somehow subverting those 'laws of equilibria' of economic theory.

All this is common sense. So why does economic theory still hold on to the imagined markets? Possibly because as economic theory has turned increasingly quantitative and technical, this crucial assumption about the behaviour of business as 'playing by the rules' has tended to be forgotten.

SABOTAGE

It is quite difficult to make sense of finance today by relying on textbook approaches, wherever their intellectual or political affinities may lie. To understand the remarkable persistence and prevalence of rogue behaviour, in this book we return to the ideas of a school of thought, often ignored nowadays, known as the old institutional economics (OIE).

Most famously associated with the works of Thorstein Veblen and John R. Commons, this body of scholarship developed in the early years of the twentieth century in the USA, a time when American capitalism was undergoing major finance-driven changes. Observing the type of economy taking hold in the late nineteenth-century USA, and which has spread around the world since, Veblen concluded, first, that the economic system of his time was defined by the figure of the businessmen and not the entrepreneur or the capitalist. And, second, that the businessmen had become true experts in sabotaging markets. In fact businessmen understand intuitively that efficient and competitive markets are likely to be good for customers, but competitive markets do not generate profits. Individually and collectively, the founding fathers of American capitalism did something about it.

Veblen saw that the new generation of businessmen that emerged in late nineteenth century were not specialist producers turned capitalists – which was essentially the way Marxists have tended to view these people. Nor were they essentially entrepreneurial or great innovators in manufacturing or organizations. Such people no doubt existed then as they do now. But they are a minority. The majority of businessmen were specialists, he thought, 'dealmakers,' experts in the art of buying and selling. Based on the evidence that he gathered largely from in-depth congressional studies of the nature of modern businesses, Veblen concluded that the successful businessmen of his day somehow found ways of making profits by interfering in markets. There was always, he found, 'something in the nature of sabotage – something in the way of retardation, restriction, withdrawal, unemployment of plant and workmen – whereby production is kept short of productive capacity'.[11] Crucially, despite the strong normative undertones to the concept, Veblen dissociated his concept of sabotage from intent, individuals or rogue behaviour. He was far more explicit in his approach than conventional economics, which suggests that market disruption is a core technique of business enterprises.

In many ways, although considered a radical, Veblen was, in effect, an early believer in efficient market theory. He also accepted that people are self-serving and individualistic. His conclusions were based not on abstraction and deduction, but on observation of actual behaviour of the great businessmen of his era. And his conclusions were that they were expert saboteurs: they knew how to ensure that market discipline does not apply to them.

We believe there is a lot to be learned from Veblen's ideas, not least because today's regulatory and institutional architecture of the leading economies was formed largely during his time. We will try to show that sabotage – or, to use Veblen's terms, something in the way of retardation, restriction, withdrawal or harming of either the clients, competitors or governments – is most probably the main source of profitability in finance and the surest way to individual bonuses and corporate profits.

We demonstrate that in each of the selected cases we study profitable transactions or 'deals' did not arise from a competitive edge in skills, capacity, expertise, hard work or superior knowledge (known as theory of asymmetrical information). Instead, they involved elements or attempts at controlling markets; that is, sabotaging the price mechanism, through either internal misrepresentation of information or facts, or predatory practices that are presently or potentially damaging to clients, competitors or the government, or a combination of all three. Specifically, what is often presented as isolated scandals in the financial system falls into one of the three categories of sabotage: sabotaging the *clients*, sabotaging *competitors* or sabotaging *governments* (or simultaneously all three). Sabotage is driven not by malice or spite, but is intended to ensure the profitability of financial trading in otherwise efficient markets.

We will try to show that by using these twin concepts of sabotage and finance as business we may achieve greater understanding of some of the otherwise inexplicable behaviour that has resulted in so many court cases, fraud investigations and hefty fines.

Perhaps the most surprising (or depressing) part of the book lies in our conclusions: very little seems to have changed since the 1920s. During that decade, a financial boom had thrived in the context of lax or missing regulations, leading to the 1929 financial crash and the Great Depression. To date, the crisis of the 1930s remains the most important period in the construction of postwar international financial and economic governance. Many of the members of Roosevelt's 'New Deal' administration in the early 1930s, such as Adolf A. Berle, Rexford G. Tugwell and other members of Roosevelt's 'Brain Trust', adopted Veblenian theory of business and its commensurate philosophy of regulation.

They were explicitly concerned with business sabotage. It is only dimly remembered today that the Glass–Steagall Act consisted of a set of regulations that were aimed at limiting the propensity towards sabotaging in finance and redirecting the financial system towards its functional purpose of mediation between savers and borrowers. The argument was presented by President Roosevelt in his first presidential address: 'The money changers have fled from their high seats in the temple of our civilization. We now restore that temple to the ancient truths.' We argue that contemporary financial regulations should return to these principles, and should incorporate the concept of sabotage in redefining and regulating the financial system in light of public welfare.

In the final part of this book we return, therefore, to the series of congressional hearings that culminated in the Pecora Report of 1934. Senator Pecora's investigation and the final report of the Senate Committee on Banking and Currency played a key role in the formulation of the Banking Act of 1933, the Securities Act of 1933 and the Securities Exchange Act of 1934, known collectively as the Glass–Steagall.

The extensive and scrupulous hearings reached the view that the crisis of 1929 was not a simple case of exuberance, mania or speculation. On the contrary, the Pecora Report, in its own words, aimed 'to expose banking operations and practices deemed detrimental to the public welfare; to reveal unsavoury and unethical methods employed in the flotation and sale of securities; and to disclose devices whereby income-tax liability is avoided or evaded'. The purpose of the report and of the ensuing regulations, it states, 'has been to lay the foundation for remedial legislation in the fields exposed'.[12]

Over time the report itself and the reason for the reform had been forgotten. The emphasis of financial governance shifted from regulations that aimed at curbing unsavoury methods of business practices, to safeguarding financial stability – and that is, we think, where the problem lies. The problems exposed during the financial crisis of 2007–9, and the seemingly never-ending stories about malfeasance or rogue behaviour in the industry tell us something about the way the business of finance is conducted. And unless regulations begin to tackle the problem of sabotage again, the problem will persist well into the future.

PART ONE

SABOTAGE AS AN ECONOMIC CONCEPT

1

——

SABOTAGE IN THE
FINANCIAL SYSTEM

'I'd rather you did not use "sabotage". Can't you find a less loaded term? Maybe, "conflicted"?' our friend the fund manager was trying to persuade us.

'I know what you mean by "sabotage", but I must say I find the word offensive. There are many hard-working, honest people who are just making a living, particularly in the lower and middle echelons of banking. Could you not find a different word?' asked an ex-BlackRock employee.

'I don't like the word "sabotage",' a former Goldman Sachs trader admitted. 'It's just harsh... Though, frankly, how else do you make money in this business... I mean, *real* money...?'

Could we have found a euphemism for 'sabotage', then? A less offensive term to describe a core technique of moneymaking in finance? We suggest not.

SABOTAGE

It was Thorstein Veblen, a father of an important school of thought in economics,[1] who first introduced sabotage as a core economic concept. 'Sabotage,' he noted, 'is a derivative of "sabot," which is French for a wooden shoe. It means going slow, with a dragging, clumsy movement, such as that manner of footgear may be expected to bring on. So [sabotage] has come to describe any manoeuvre of slowing-down, inefficiency, bungling, obstruction.'[2] By the late nineteenth century the meaning of sabotage was used more widely in American popular parlance:

> to cover all such peaceable or surreptitious manoeuvres of delay, obstruction, friction, and defeat, whether employed by the workmen to enforce their claims, or by the employers to defeat their employees, or by competitive business concerns to get the better of their business rivals or to secure their own advantage.[3]

Veblen believed that in this expanded meaning the term 'sabotage' captured an important dimension of modern business.

Thorstein Veblen is a controversial figure in the history of economic thought. His writing style is archaic, quite convoluted and always political. His legacy is mostly associated with *The Theory of the Leisure Class*, a critique of consumerism and social divisions in capitalism which he published in 1899. Today, Veblen's theories are rarely taught in university programmes; global search engines yield many more results for 'John Maynard Keynes' and 'John Commons' than they do for 'Thorstein Veblen'.

Yet in the wake of the 2007–9 crisis, and in light of the revelations of the Panama and Paradise dossiers and the like, one unavoidably begins to ponder whether Veblen's theory of sabotage is relevant for making sense of the many apparent crises in the capitalist organization. In today's business world, and particularly in that most lucrative yet most competitive of all sectors, the financial system, the practices of deploying all the means available may offer a better insight into the actual business of finance than conventional theories of market and economic behaviour do. By 'all means available' we do mean all means available, including innovation, obstruction, undercutting, impairing, damaging, vandalizing and cheating – generally within the letter but not in the spirit of the law, and sometimes beyond the limits of the law altogether.

Now, not everyone would agree with the very premise that the financial system is, in fact, a competitive market. It is much more difficult to start a bank than, say, a restaurant: one not only needs some serious starting capital but, crucially, a set of licences from the state which are very hard to obtain in most jurisdictions. To start trading as a hedge fund, one needs to have a number of well-endowed subscribers, proprietary strategy and, again, starting capital. The insurance sector is heavily regulated too. In other words, theoretically, the apparent high barriers to entry and a degree of market concentration mean that the financial system is not a competitive market.

In the real world, however, functionally and geographically, competition in finance is tough. Since the late 1960s, technology has increased the dynamism of the financial dealings and vastly expanded the range and scope of financial institutions. These changes put pressure on the older inhabitants of finance. Existing banks compete fiercely with one another and face challenges from new entrants to the sector: all major supermarkets today offer a range of financial services and products that were traditionally the prerogative of the banks. Geographically, too, the breakdown of national regulations and the rise of emerging market economies has widely expanded the number and the range of financial institutions, with the majority now operating across several jurisdictions, time zones and asset classes.

In 1997 Paul Volcker, formerly the chairman of the Federal Reserve, reflected on this heightened competition. Even in the face of the intense and growing pressures of competition, Volcker noted, 'The industry never has been so profitable'. The noted anomaly would later become known as Volcker's paradox, and would refer to the seemingly strange coexistence of intense competition and historically high profit rates in commercial banking.[4] Why was this a puzzle for one of the leading economic figures of his generation?

To resolve Volcker's paradox, and to understand Veblen's theory of sabotage, we need to turn to the dilemma of profitability.

THE DILEMMA OF PROFITABILITY

There is no better way to start than with an idea that is taught to every student of economics around their third, or perhaps fourth, week of Economics 101. After learning about the workings of the price mechanism in competitive markets and the behaviour of (rather selfish) utility-maximizing consumers, students are usually directed to a chapter called 'Market Equilibrium under Perfect Competition'. There they discover, alas, that it is next to impossible for firms to make profits in perfectly competitive markets.

Here comes one of the greatest ironies of economics. The theory widely used to introduce market reforms in the name of greater efficiencies and individual wealth in fact shows, compellingly, that although the main motivation of economic agents is to make money, in a properly functioning market they hardly make any money at all. In his 1941 study Joe Bain writes: 'In a purely competitive market, where there is free entry and competitive buying of factors, long-run equilibrium returns for all firms should just cover contractual and imputed wages, interest, and rent.'[5] In other words, in an efficient open market, firms are likely to make very thin profits, just enough to ensure the survival of the business. If the theory is correct, then it is obviously a problem for businesses.

Unsurprisingly, many bright minds have strived to understand how a market economy can continue to function in conditions of low profitability. Could it be that businesses consist of irrepressibly optimistic people, blind to the futility of their efforts? A while ago, Veblen suggested they are not. 'The experts in buying and selling', as he called them, never believed in markets in the first place, certainly not in competitive markets. They believed, instead, in controlling the market. By whatever means possible.

It would take a bit longer for mainstream economists to reach a broadly similar conclusion, albeit with polite refrain from the negative connotations associated with terms such as sabotage. The subsequent revision yielded two ideas. One was offered by Kenneth Arrow, the Nobel laureate. Inquiring into the nature of the market, Arrow argued that conventional models of the economy are flawed because they assume companies to be passive agents, where 'each individual participant...is supposed to take prices as given and determine his choices as to purchase and sales accordingly'.[6] In reality, he says, market participants are not passive at all; they try to turn the tables on the market and become not price takers, but price givers.

How do they do it? Our students of Economics 101 do not have to go far in search of an appropriate strategy. Around week five or six of their course, they learn that being a sole supplier in the market, or a monopolist, is the ideal form of price-giving technique. Market participants seek monopoly to achieve a degree of control over the prices to the consumer. If monopoly is unattainable, firms can try and attain the next best thing: they can group together to form something that resembles a monopoly. In doing so they may gain what the economics profession calls 'excess profits'.[7]

Monopoly should not be confused with another form associated with large size; that is, economies of scale. Economies of scale – efficiencies gained from being a large structure – can be driven by genuine reasons. They help businesses achieve reduction in unit costs. This is the case, for instance, with large and complex conglomerates. Let us consider the cosmetics giant L'Oréal as an example of the difference between controlling markets and economies of scale. On a pharmacy or department store shelf, L'Oréal products are sold on a designated stand, often next to Maybelline, Bourgeois and, say, Vichy. But L'Oréal itself owns most of what appear to be its market 'competitors', including Lancôme, Giorgio Armani Beauty, Helena Rubinstein, Decleor, Vichy, Maybelline, La Roche-Posay and many more. L'Oréal is able, therefore, to share heavy research costs and facilities that underpin various products sold under a range of its different brands. Put differently, L'Oréal successfully builds on the economies of scale. Or, at least, this is what our Economics 101 textbook suggests.

In reality L'Oréal achieved these economies of scale largely through mergers and acquisitions. And in acquiring its competitors across different market segments, L'Oréal has attained something that has nothing to do with economies of scale. By controlling different brands L'Oréal can now determine the degree to which Vichy competes on prices with Maybelline, or Lancôme with Helena Rubinstein and Giorgio Armani Beauty. The 'utility maximizing' consumer of economic theory is presented as someone who would rationally make choices between these competing brands on perceived quality and price. In the meantime the parent, L'Oréal, has undertaken strategic and tactical steps to ensure that those choices are not made in the free market of abstract theory, but in the industry where L'Oréal decides many of the parameters. L'Oréal does not own all cosmetics brands. But it is powerful enough to ensure that when a new brand achieves a degree of following among customers, L'Oréal is in position, together with its bankers, to buy that brand. In classic Veblenian terms, L'Oréal sabotages its competitors, customers and the market itself.

The second route to controlling the price level is more targeted. Theoretically, a solution to the profitability quandary may lie not in the structure of the market per se, but in the specifics of its behaviour. This idea originates in the pro-market Hayekian vision and is based on the notion of temporary disequilibria. The theory suggests that by inventing a new product or innovating a new service – and often gaining protection for the product under patent and rules of intellectual property rights,[8] business can achieve a temporary monopoly in the newly created market. Some free-market economists conclude, therefore, that one can make profit in a competitive market only through innovation, a process to be nurtured and encouraged.

There is no shortage of advice on how to do just that on bookshop shelves and online. There are, for instance, quantitative suggestions. Here, the competitive edge and high profits can be delivered by a sophisticated command of financial engineering and scientific precision in management. In the world of business studies the profitability conundrum can be resolved by strategic moves. Here, Keith Ward's highly popular manual, now into its fourth edition, offers a typical solution:

> In order to create this value, the company has to develop and then exploit one or more sustainable competitive advantages, which will allow it to earn super profits on a continuing basis. Most modern sustainable competitive advantages are the result of the successful implementation of marketing strategies (e.g. brand building, customer loyalty development, market segmentation).[9]

It is an elegant argument. It would be even more persuasive if it were believable.

What is there in the organization of the market that ensures businesses will concentrate only on innovation, and overlook all the other tools in the Veblenian arsenal of sabotage? Well, nothing, really. It is only the state, scorned and despised by Hayekians, that is in a position to try and do something about sabotage. Liberals are quick to point out that government officials are bent on rent seeking and are often corrupt (that is, they are corrupted by the very businesses whose freedom of action these liberals espouse). The free market of neoliberals, in contrast, is supposed to encourage innovation, as admittedly it did to an extent. In reality, however, the freer the market, the more 'deregulated' it is, the wider the scope for sabotage.

Whatever theoretical or pragmatic arguments about competition there may be, one thing is becoming apparent: no business wants to be anywhere near the point of equilibrium in a competitive market. 'A perfect competitor will do whatever he can to increase his gain: bargaining vigorously with others for a better deal, innovating new products if he sees a profit to doing so, strategically misrepresenting his private information if this is profitable.'[10]

THE BUSINESS WORLD OF THORSTEIN VEBLEN

So, how do businesses make money in competitive markets? Through sabotage, was a bold answer Veblen offered to a question that few had asked in his day. Veblen's choice of language here is hardly scientific. Yet in adopting a colloquialism of his day, and weaving it into economic theory, Veblen had a much more profound point in mind than a mere argument about business opportunism. To understand the deeper and more lasting implications of the theory, we need to look back at one of the long-running disputes in economics: the one between the analytical and historical schools.

To this day, economics is dominated by the analytical school. This particular approach has sought, in effect, to replicate economic conditions in the scientist's lab. The fundamental assumption underlying most economic modelling is simple enough. Since we cannot bring real economic life into the lab, we can replicate the real world as a thought process, a set of imagined scenarios constructed through a logical chain of abstractions and generalizations. Thus, in our thought process, we can describe the economy as a 'marketplace', an abstraction based on an analogy with a seasonal farmers' market. The market is a meeting place where buyers and sellers would meet each other, bargain and reach a resolution which determines the price of the product. In this thought process, economic agents are a fairly homogenous mass: they are self-centred, rational, 'utility maximizing' and risk-averse individuals. A banker or manufacturer would always seek to sell at a highest price possible and thus maximize profit. On the other hand, buyers (consumers) are also self-centred 'utility maximizing' agents. They would naturally seek to pay least for manufactured goods or financial products.

In a fundamental way the market of economic theory is a form of decentralized democracy, where everyone has an equal vote. Theory then develops through puzzling encounters between imagined and real marketplace. Over time, it evolved to accommodate a more sophisticated set of arguments to fine-tune core assumptions.

Veblen would probably agree that individuals or corporate entities are self-centred, likely to be keen on maximizing profits and minimizing payments. But his fundamental method of analysis was different. He developed his theories as generalizations not from the assumptions about abstracted individuals and their likely behaviour, but, rather, from observations of the concrete actions of businesses and the corporate sector. Veblen was not an empiricist: he did not study the corporations directly. Instead, his ideas were shaped primarily by a series of incisive congressional investigative reports into the behaviour of business in the fledgling American corporate economy of the late nineteenth and early twentieth centuries.

Studying these reports in depth, Veblen discerned growing tension between two groups of people in the business world. On the one side there were the owners and main shareholders of large companies; Veblen called them 'absentee owners'. On the other side there were people he described as the 'managers' and the 'engineers' who actually ran those companies. Veblen noted that the two groups had fundamentally different aspirations for the business, made different contributions to running the companies, and had divergent outlooks on the nature of business. These differences were at the heart of the conflict between the 'absentee owners' and the 'engineers'.

To Veblen, the engineer and the manager brought something uniquely positive to modern capitalism. They invented and perfected techniques of manufacturing and distribution that allowed humans, perhaps for the first time in history, to be less reliant on the vagaries of mother nature. But he also observed that the new American capitalism of the late nineteenth century was increasingly being defined by very large businesses. The new companies and factories were controlled by business owners, or the 'captains of industry', as they were called, who worked closely with the great financial houses like J. P. Morgan and the Rockefellers' Chase. The 'captains of industry' knew little about the specifics of the products they sold. They did not seem to possess managerial or practical skills; nor were they interested in the day-to-day running of businesses.

So what exactly did J. P. Morgan, the Rockefellers and the financial houses, together with the 'captains of industry', bring to the business? Not very much, thought Veblen. They were the dealmakers, experts 'in the art of buying and selling'. The economic environment for these 'captains of industry', the businessmen, was not the abstracted 'marketplace' of the economist. Instead, it involved a very real and tangible world of clients and potential clients, other businesses, the regulators and lawmakers, the states and, increasingly, the federal state. As Veblen reasoned, these businesses, or 'competitive business concerns', would do whatever was necessary 'to get the better of their business rivals or to secure their own advantage' vis-à-vis clients, potential clients or the state. By 'all means' Veblen did mean all means, including innovation, reorganization and efficiency improvements, but also obstruction, friction, lying, impairing and even the use of force. They were 'unremittingly engaged in a routine of acquisition, in which they habitually reach[ed] their ends by a shrewd restriction of output'.[11] 'Restricting competition, not improving efficiency, was the primary purpose in organizing trusts, accomplished by either buying out competitors or crushing them by merciless competition and unscrupulous predatory tactics'.[12]

In short, what the captains of industry were experts in was sabotage.

KNOWLEDGE, POWER AND OTHER PEOPLE'S MONEY

Thorstein Veblen was not a friend of the financial industry. If he was critical of the new capitalists of his day generally, he was specifically hostile to the bankers. He saw them as mere 'experts in prices and profits and financial manoeuvres' who preyed upon the more creative and innovative aspects of modern industry. 'With no competent grasp of the industrial arts,' he wrote, 'they continue to exercise a plenary discretion as captains of industry'.[13]

Meanwhile, Veblen also noted that the daily operations in finance were being increasingly routinized, which led him to conclude that finance was 'best to be taken care of by a clerical staff of trained accountants'.[14] The standardization of financial services appeared to contrast with the superprofits made by large banking groups. Veblen reasoned that in the environment of growing standardization and routine, the great control achieved by large financial houses, and the great profits they were making, had little to do with business acumen. The financiers capitalized on the great economies of scale in the industry and the fact that society and the markets expanded. 'So the corporation financier, as a class, came in for an "unearned increment" of income, on the simple plan of "sitting tight".'[15]

There was more to it. Three additional factors made finance particularly disruptive in modern society. The first fundamental problem was that, as the title of a famous book published in 1914 implies,[16] the sector specialized in making money by using other people's money (OPM).[17] And so an unavoidable conflict defined the relationship between financial houses and their clients: the more the clients benefited from the arrangement, the less did the financial houses, and vice versa. Of course, it could be argued that the smart financial houses would take a long-term view of their business and look after all their clients' interests (otherwise clients would desert them in favour of other intermediaries). But, to Veblen, the evidence suggested that financial houses were rather short-term in outlook. They would rather make money to-day than cultivate long-term relationships with clients for the future. As we will see later in this book, nothing much had changed since Veblen's times, and sabotaging clients remains a big and profitable venture in the business of finance.

Second, since the financial houses made their money by using other people's money, they had great vested interest in maximizing the amount of money they controlled. The more OPM they controlled, the more they could potentially have gained. In principle, to play in this high-stakes game, you could use your own funds. But for a large economy like that of the US, your own funds tend to be insufficient. You need to leverage control over a serious portion of industry and the sector to be a meaningful

FIGURE 1.1.

Ownership and control-pyramid structure

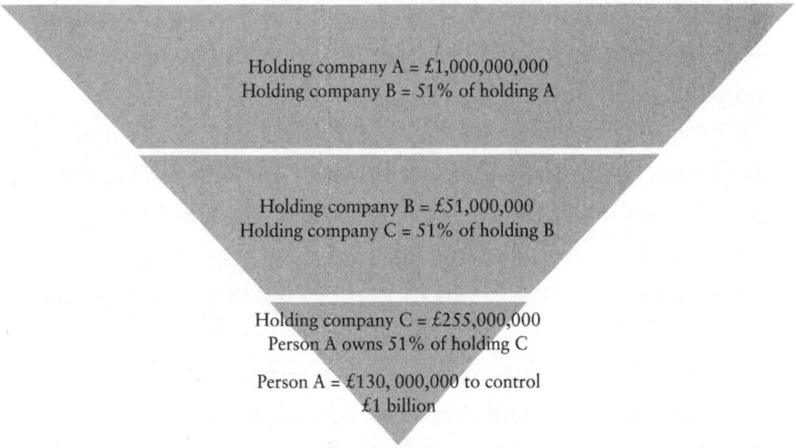

Holding company A = £1,000,000,000
Holding company B = 51% of holding A

Holding company B = £51,000,000
Holding company C = 51% of holding B

Holding company C = £255,000,000
Person A owns 51% of holding C

Person A = £130, 000,000 to control
£1 billion

player in the high-stakes game of sabotage. And so the technique of pyramid control through holding companies was perfected.

A simple version of such a structure would resemble the diagram above. In a three-layer pyramidal structure a holding of £130m can be easily leveraged to control £1bn.

The more sophisticated versions of such holdings would use loans and bonds to leverage control. In a three-tiered pyramidal structure (Figure 1.2) $5m could easily be leveraged to $1bn of asset control. The practice was so common that by the 1920s J. P. Morgan alone was estimated to have controlled, in one way or another, a quarter of the industrial assets of the US.[18] Presidents and entire administrations would line up with one of these houses against the other. These banking houses created cartels, trusts and combinations to maintain higher prices for products, used their financial power to intimidate and compel competitors, and would not shy away from influencing the political system.[19]

Pyramidal holding companies gave financiers and absentee owners enormous leverage over great swathes of the American economy.

And so leverage and control became active tools in the bankers' arsenal of sabotage. The power of these tools was further amplified through unique knowledge about the entities the leverage links conveyed to the financiers. 'The banker occupies the pilot-room of the capitalist system. Because of his intimate connection with his clients the banker is easily in a position to "know all, see all, hear all".[20] J. P. Morgan & Co., for instance, sat on 167 diversified company directorships.[21] By controlling so many assets, and by having a seat at the table, the bankers obtained knowledge of what was going on. They used this knowledge to learn about the health of these companies, about market conditions, about possibilities for monopolies and combinations, and generally about opportunities for sabotage. 'Through a maze of financial detail, opposing claims, debts, spurious loans of broken or plundered enterprises, the Corsair [the reference here is to the legendary J. P. Morgan Sr] and his lieutenants moved irresistibly to impose order "upon conditions of his own".[22]

The Senate Committee on Banking and Currency, set up in 1932 to investigate the causes of the 1929 financial crisis, and known as the Pecora Commission Congressional Investigation, devoted considerable space to studying the 'art of leveraging' and, specifically, the use of holding companies' pyramidal structures, which it viewed as a key contributing factor to the 1929 crisis. The Pecora committee concluded that the big financial houses were really not interested in the daily running of these companies. The committee addressed the issue directly with J. P. Morgan Jr. 'It is difficult to perceive,' wrote the authors of the report, 'how the members of the firm of J. P. Morgan & Co., with 167

FIGURE 1.2.

Ownership and control-pyramid structure 2

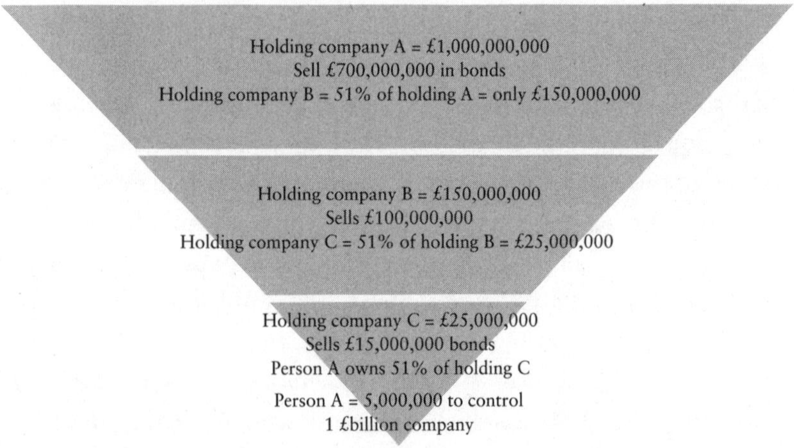

Holding company A = £1,000,000,000
Sell £700,000,000 in bonds
Holding company B = 51% of holding A = only £150,000,000

Holding company B = £150,000,000
Sells £100,000,000
Holding company C = 51% of holding B = £25,000,000

Holding company C = £25,000,000
Sells £15,000,000 bonds
Person A owns 51% of holding C

Person A = 5,000,000 to control
1 £billion company

diversified directorships... could adequately fulfil their directorial duties.' J. P. Morgan Jr confirmed this. As he told the commission: 'It can be no director's duty to run the company. It must be the duty of the executives. The duty of the board is not to run the company and mess into the little details of running it.'[23]

Nearly a century later, this has not changed either. As we will see further in this book, high leverage and sheer size remain among the most common sabotaging techniques in modern finance.

Veblen's theory of sabotage was only a reflection of practices well known at his time. For him, sabotage was predicated on the ongoing conflict between, on the one hand, absentee owners – the big shareholders and the financial houses – who used financial instruments to control businesses; and the engineers and managers, on the other. He believed that these absentee owners, organized by the large financial houses, were experts in the arts of buying, selling and sabotage. They leveraged their power and control through a system of pyramidal holding companies. They always wanted to have a seat at the table, not to improve the daily running of businesses, but to learn the business strategy, to understand where the weak points were, and where to attack and sabotage. To this end, they used their powerful position across the industry and strategic control of other people's money.

THE NEW LIBERALS

During the 1970s, new answers to the profitability conundrum began to gain traction. These were suggested by the new liberals, the followers of Ludwig von Mises and Friedrich Hayek. Like other economists, the liberals did accept that there was a fundamental problem with profits in competitive market conditions. Their argument, however, was that these problems could be turned into positive solutions. Due to the profitability conundrum, they reasoned, successful businesses, including in finance, had no choice but to innovate and change. And the more they innovated, the more they contributed to economic growth and social welfare. Competitive markets were a great force for good.

During the period of low economic growth of the 1970s, the liberals regained many supporters. Armed with their theory of competitive innovation, they seemed to have all the answers to the puzzle of stagflation.[24] Let competition do its job, they argued; free the markets and unleash the forces of innovation, and the benefits would show in no time. The liberals viewed with suspicion the managers and the engineers whom Veblen had celebrated. Their suspicion had logic behind it. Mainly interested in the status quo, the managers were bureaucratic and slow to accept change. They colluded with workers' organizations in order to have it easy. Managers were seeking life-time employment and cushy jobs. To the liberal, managers were the culprits of the economic problem: they slowed down competition, stifled innovation and thus, ultimately, impeded progress.

In contrast, the liberals pointed that shareholders – Veblen's 'absentee owners' – had a different attitude to innovation. Shareholders were not involved in the daily running of businesses, and had no chance to collude with workers. Shareholders were interested only in profits and cared not about the comfort of either the workforce or the managers. By introducing 'shareholder value' to American capitalism the liberals advocated a system that would be specifically oriented towards short-term profits. The shorter, the better; shareholder value imposed fierce competition in the marketplace. Competitive markets, the liberal believed, would force innovation and change. Shareholder value was positive. Profits were central. Greed was good.

The argument quickly evolved into a disciplinary and political debate. Veblenians believed that Hayek and his disciples ignored a crucial point. Owners and shareholders did not innovate in any way, either in industry or in finance. Their mentality, their 'habit of thought', was that of sabotage. If liberals hoped that by introducing short-termism through shareholder value the shareholders would force reluctant managers and engineers to innovate, Veblenians thought the new liberal era would simply give licence to increased sabotage on a massive scale. For the liberals, deregulation was the battle cry against 'red tape' of bureaucracy which would stifle innovation. For Veblenians, 'deregulation' meant that the rules which were introduced as checks against the sabotaging tendencies in capitalism and the financial system were now removed. With the inevitable consequence to the clients, competitors, governments and, eventually, the system itself.

GLOBALIZATION

The 1990s saw the rise of the references to sabotage, albeit mentioned under different synonyms. Techniques originally described by Veblen in the 1920s–1930s began to appear in academic studies as well as memoirs of finance professionals.[25] One area of rising concern was commercial banking. In the process of making and monitoring the loans, commercial banks became privy to information about their clients that was not generally known to external investors. Some studies reported that a number of commercial banks underwrote securities they privately knew were questionable, and then used the proceeds from the issue to pay down the loans they had issued. In this way those banks could protect their own interests at the expense of outside investors in the newly issued securities.[26]

Some sixty years before, similar incidences were recorded in the US by the Pecora Committee hearings. The Glass–Steagall Act of 1933 prohibited national banks from engaging in securities activities, either directly or through affiliates, precisely to avoid such practices. But in 1987 certain provisions of Glass–Steagall were relaxed, with some banks (for example, J. P. Morgan and Bankers Trust Co.) allowed to set up Section 20 subsidiaries that could underwrite securities. These were supposedly subject to 'firewalls': that is, no communication with the parent bank was allowed. Further deregulations were proposed later.

The 1990s brought into light a myriad of cases involving conflict of interest. Investment banks which sought lucrative underwriting business would sometimes attract issuers with favourable analyst research coverage. 'Analyst research departments came under the sway of investment bankers, with analyst compensation often being determined by investment banking business generally, or even based upon specific deals.'[27] In other words, researchers and analysts, whether working for the investment bank or for an outside consultancy, had a material interest in providing favourable assessments of the deal irrespective of the truth.

Another area of conflict is the financial advisers and investment funds. Financial advisers are supposed to provide unbiased advice best suited to the clients' needs and interests. But often, in the drive for higher commission fees, they would steer investors into products that bore higher costs and unnecessary risk.[28] Similarly, mortgage advisers do not benefit from *not* selling a mortgage. Even if they know the client may be putting themselves into great hardship by entering into a mortgage agreement, or even if they know the borrower is likely to be unable to pay, mortgage advisers have an incentive to try and persuade the clients to take a mortgage, and help them present their affairs in such a way that mortgage companies would issue the mortgages. Aware of such conflicts of interest, mortgage companies, in turn, devised schemes for passing the mortgages on to others. Enabled by the policies of deregulation and centred on the use of sophisticated financial engineering, these techniques transformed the financial system from the kind that Veblen analysed at the dawn of finance capitalism to its modern incarnation. Despite the great transformation, however, sabotage remains a central principle of business making in finance in the twenty-first century.

Veblen wrote about industrial sabotage focusing on the business processes of the late nineteenth and early twentieth centuries.

Sabotage in the Financial System

Today's financial markets are very different from the ones of Veblen's day. The forms of sabotage in the financial system have changed and evolved over time. The principle, however, has remained: if you want to make money – *real* money – in finance, you need to find ways of sabotaging either your clients, your competitors or the government. If you are big enough, you can succeed on all three fronts.

2

——

WE ALL ARE IN IT TOGETHER

Sabotage and the Cycle of Debt

Will Emerson, a senior bank executive played by Paul Bettany in the movie *Margin Call*, explains the function of banking to a younger colleague, who is about to lose his job in the upcoming financial meltdown:

> If people want to live like this... with their big cars and these houses that they haven't even paid for. Then you are necessary. The only reason they can continue to live like kings is because we've got our fingers on the scale in THEIR favor. And if I were to take my finger off... Then the whole world gets really fucking fair, really fucking quickly. And no one wants that, they say they do... but they don't. They want what we're giving them, but they also want to play innocent and pretend they have no idea

how we get it. And that's more hypocrisy than I can swallow. So fuck 'em![1]

Will Emerson is hardly a great theorist. But he is today's incarnation of the 'big picture' businessman Veblen wrote about a century ago. Lacking a deep understanding of the complex financial instruments his bank was selling to clients, Will can nonetheless pinpoint, with surgical precision, something that often gets lost in academic essays or bestselling memoirs about the apparently deviant behaviour in the industry: Will Emerson knows that society needs people like Emerson.

Deep in the workings of the financial system, the Will Emersons of this world are making sure that our individual debts are aggregated into credit flows that keep the economy going. They undertake the complex financial alchemy that sustains mountains of debt which are at the very heart of the modern economy. We all – households, businesses, governments, corporations – are small-moving particles of this system. Yet rarely do we appreciate either how central debt is – its creation and tradability – to our daily life, or the actual role the Will Emersons of this world play for us.

This oversight is a result of many doctrinal and political factors. Most of our knowledge about debt comes from theories that see debt within the frame of Robinson Crusoe economics. In that world, debt – just like any other economic category – is an individuated property: a quantity borrowed for a time from someone else that has to be repaid. It is the individual who borrows that is ultimately responsible for the debt repayment. As debt must be paid back, the debtor will have fewer funds available in the future. The more we borrow now, the more we take away from future generations. We are advised to reduce our debt. Throughout history, a sophisticated mythology has been built around this particular doctrine of debt.[2] The doctrine is not entirely wrong, but it is not entirely correct either. Many of its implications can be very misleading.

Our point in this chapter is to argue that as the nature of debt has changed, and as society has become ever more dependent on financial wizardry for the cycle of debt to continue, finance has achieved a uniquely powerful position in society. Susan Strange, a great critic of finance, called this position 'structural power'.[3] It is a position that Will Emerson and his colleagues would know how to leverage so that they can sabotage everyone around to ensure the ongoing profitability of their businesses.

How did we get here?

FUTURITY

Perhaps the best way to understand the complexity of modern debt is by pondering a core question in economics: Do financial markets create wealth? Or do they simply transfer wealth from one part of the system to another?

The textbook answer to this question suggests that the financial markets transfer (or allocate) capital to underinvested segments of the economy. This answer implies that, on its own, finance does not create wealth: real wealth is created elsewhere, by real people sweating it out in the real economy. What finance does is provide an important *service* to the real, productive economy, and hence to society, by allocating the necessary funds to those who can create wealth, while denying funds to those who are unlikely to generate it.

This theory received a theoretical backup known as the efficient market theory (EMT). In 1970 Eugene Francis Fama, described on his Wikipedia page as 'The Father of Finance',[4] argued in a now classic article, that 'the primary role of the capital market is allocation of ownership of the economy's capital stock'. In general terms, he continues, 'a market in which prices always "fully reflect" available information is called "efficient".'[5] In turn, to fully reflect available information and fulfil its core service function of allocating capital efficiently, the financial market should be as free as possible from external interference.

Intuitively, this theory of finance as mere service economy makes sense. But, surprisingly, it is the wrong answer. It comes from the paradigm which, for the sake of simplicity, we would call 'the economics of the past'.[6] The economics of the past is predicated on the assumption that the capital that the financial markets transfer between borrowers and savers already exists, having been accumulated as a product of past economic activity. For instance, the carpenter makes tables and chairs which he then sells in the market. The carpenter then deposits his profits in the bank. The bank, in turn, lends those funds to a different borrower – playing the role of the intermediator between the saver and the borrower. In a freely competitive market, Fama tells us, the allocation of funds will be performed as efficiently as humanly possible.

For some types of savings in some contexts, such a perspective may hold true. But for most advanced capitalist economies, the process of capital allocation does not work in the sequence described above – and the difference in sequencing of debt creation has enormous implications. In reality the financial system is not waiting patiently until sufficient savings get accumulated before it begins to allocate resources. Instead, capital is created anew by banks and financial markets whenever they are able to identify a new lending opportunity or create an asset.

In fact the financial system does not allocate resources, but, for lack of a better description, creates resources literally out of thin air. The major function of the financial markets today is to identify an activity that can be converted into an economic asset (i.e., identify an activity that can generate revenues), and to enable this new financial asset to be created (by pricing this activity and facilitating a market for it). Banks create credit anew, against future income streams of those they lend capital to. Despite appearances, both these vital functions – determining a creditworthiness of a business or borrower and determining to what extent an activity can be viable and profitable – have little to do with the economics of the past. Instead, they have everything to do with the security of expectations about a potential borrower, an asset or a market. Or, as John R. Commons puts it, with *futurity*.

Over the centuries, finance has developed sophisticated mechanisms that allow it to harvest income from the future. Cumulatively, these mechanisms have evolved into an economy of futurity. In the economics of futurity, credit, or debt, is not simply transferred from one person to another; rather, new credit lines are drawn against the future. If, say, Apple promises to sell a new generation of iPhones next year, Apple would borrow funds today against the income generated by the next iPhone. Indeed, Apple can borrow against the income stream generated by the next two, three or more generations of iPhones, and this credit line will be deployed almost instantly, not having to wait until the next iPhone is created, generating purchasing power in the economy.

The notion of borrowing from the future is not unique to the economic system. Physics talks about matter and antimatter as borrowing from the future. And just like in physics, where this process is very complex, such borrowing from the future is not a simple affair. In fact the precision involved in valuing futurity requires a great degree of technical and fundamental knowledge, coordination among many moving parts, balance, expertise, audacity and, last but not least, start-up capital. This delicate process of coordination of a system of borrowing and paying back the future is organized by the gatekeepers, the Will Emersons of the financial system. And the more complex, technically challenging and opaque this process of coordination of borrowing against the future is, the more opportunities there are to sabotage clients, governments and, often, each other.

A HISTORY OF FUTURITY

So, what is this system of futurity and where does it come from? The history of futurity goes a long way back. Already in the early days of agriculture and trade, humans turned to credit innovations to protect themselves from the unknowns of the future.[7] Promises to pay (or buy) or guarantees to repay a loan taken, say, in silver with sesame seeds at a going rate in the future were used in trading nations of the ancient Middle East. Carved on clay tablets, such trading contracts were found in ancient Mesopotamia, Hellenistic Egypt and the Roman Empire. These contracts were typically negotiated privately; many were not recorded on the books. Often, they were not even named on those clay tablets, suggesting that contemporaries did not recognize their significance as financial instruments. They do resemble, however, what today we call forward contracts, a type of a financial derivative.[8]

Historians believe that such forward financial derivatives spread along the early trading and migration routes. They proliferated in Europe during the Renaissance.[9] Over time, and responding to societal needs, forward contracts would become more sophisticated. Farmers, for instance, plant seeds at the beginning of the season, but reap what they sow only at the end of the season. They then bring their products to the market and convert them to cash. Farmers have to invest, therefore, a few months before they are able to get the rewards. For the poor farmer, those few months are critical: bad weather or infestation can destroy the entire crop. Between seasons, the farmer bore the cost of investment and the risk (of the quality of the crop and the price when completed).

At this point a financier would intervene. He would buy the future crop, the one that is yet to be sown, thus taking some of the investment and risk away from the farmer. The farmer would sign a contract with the financier for the delivery of the crop at the end of the season. In many instances the creditor would also loan the farmer some money to invest. Increasingly, agriculture became commercialized through the mechanisms of such forward financial derivatives contracts.

Similar arrangements evolved in other sectors. Around the tenth century, commercial partnership contracts for sea or land ventures, the *commandas*, emerged. One partner to the venture would put up the money for the voyage, and the other travelled on the venture. Many such contracts could be considered as commodity forward contracts, where in exchange for the invested capital the 'venturer' agreed to acquire specified commodities.[10] In this way futurity-oriented instruments were crucial financial innovations because they helped people manage the uncertainty associated with trading and agricultural activities, and because they ensured that the capital invested through the loan was directed to the economic activity itself – farming, trading or sea explorations.

It did not take long for what is today called a 'secondary' market, or market for securities, to emerge. At an early stage the traders who bought those future contracts insisted on the delivery of goods, which they would warehouse and trade. Over time, however, they realized that this was not necessary. They could simply hold and sell those forward financial contracts without having much to do with the product themselves. The contracts became, in effect, independent financial products. Financiers would bundle these forward contracts and sell them to others, spreading the risk associated with such contracts more widely. The possessor of these contracts, whether an original party to the contract or a purchaser of the contract in the secondary market, had a claim, a right, over some future income streams – say, the future income that so many bushels of wheat will yield. '

The rise and spread of future contracts and financial interests would generate a massive institutional change. With the functioning market for contracts, physical products such as crops were abstracted and turned into tradable financial 'assets' – underpinning the rise of trade in property rights. Traders stopped holding on to products not only because they realized they did not have to but because, over time, they began to associate riches and wealth with the contracts themselves. Wealth, which for centuries had a strong tangible flavour (embodied in wheat, land, corn or exotic spices), was transformed, in effect, into an entirely abstract concept: *a contract*.

This marked a radical change in how wealth was perceived and materialized. For centuries, demonstrable wealth had been visualized with the aid of a rare metal. As the great medievalist scholar J. Huizinga tells us, the wealth of Philip the Good could be placed in heavy boxes of gold:

> Philip the Good knew the political language which the people understand. To convince the Hollanders and Frisians that he was perfectly able to conquer the bishopric of Utrecht, he exhibits, during the festivities of The Hague, in 1456, precious plate to the value of thirty thousand silver marks. Everybody may come and look at it. Amongst other things, two hundred thousand gold lions have been brought from Lille contained in two chests which every one may try to lift up. The demonstration of the solvency of the state took the form of an entertainment at a fair.[11]

But with the development of new financial instruments, wealth could now be captured by symbols, ownership rights over contractual obligations. A wealthy person could simply point to a pile of contracts on his desk to demonstrate how wealthy he was. What these future contracts meant is that the possessor of these contracts had a right over some future income stream. In a simple form it could be a claim on the future income that so many bushels of wheat would yield. Or what owners of financial derivatives could show was that they had a right and a claim over the behaviour of those future claims. They could get, for instance, all the income that would be generated if a bushel of wheat was sold above a certain threshold. If the price went really high, they would make a lot of money; if not, they might lose their fortunes. By speculating on those contracts they had created demand for future contracts, ensuring that primary traders in future contracts would potentially have more capital at their disposal to purchase agricultural and trading contracts. This meant, in turn, that farmers and traders received more credit from those primary traders.

These were truly momentous shifts: the slow-moving European economy began its journey towards capitalism.[12]

FUTURITY IN THE AGE OF MANUFACTURING

As technology evolved and manufacturing took centre stage in the economy, financial products evolved as well. In principle a buyer could purchase a 'future' manufacturing good, that is, products yet to be made. But that did not really make sense. Banks extended loans to manufacturing enterprises in the belief they would generate returns by selling their products to the market. Their investment, however, was not exactly in the product. Rather, the investment went to the manufacturing entity, the firm, which would produce the product. Similarly, buyers were more interested in purchasing shares in enterprises, as in the seventeenth century with traders like the East India Company. To buy a share in an enterprise is to buy a claim over the future income stream of that enterprise.

The idea of advancing credit against future income streams became established. Banks or individual investors would assess the potential for future income streams of a manufacturing unit on the basis of all sorts of considerations: quality of the machinery, the nature of the market, but also quality of organization, access to unique technology and ability of companies to create a following among their customers. Investors took a holistic approach to manufacturing units, which they treated as 'going concerns'. They recognized that in addition to tangible assets, going concerns possessed many assets that were intangible, such as know-how, technology, intellectual property rights, organizational capacity, reputation, corporate culture and so on.

This portion of the value of the entity was called 'goodwill'. In a short space of time, goodwill began to account for a considerable amount of investment in companies. For instance, during the establishment of the US Steel Trust in 1901, about half of its capitalization of $1.4bn was attributable to goodwill. Indeed, by 1907 Goldman of Goldman and Sachs would hit on the idea of generating ideational goodwill value out of the mostly family-owned enterprises in the US at the time. He went on a road tour to persuade families to capitalize their 'entrepreneurial value' as goodwill by doing IPOs. Quite literally, the very idea of goodwill and the notion of companies as going concerns would generate additional funding from banks or individuals.

During an early phase of these developments, between the 1880s and the 1920s, valuation of companies as going concerns was based on a distinction between 'tangible' and 'intangible' value of the business, or between the real, physical goods or land owned by the firm, as opposed to the more ethereal goodwill. Firms would issue two types of shares: preferred shares related to the tangible value of those companies, and common shares (sometimes called entrepreneurial shares), issued against the perceived intangible value of the company. From a financial or business perspective, however, the distinction became blurred. Manufacturing and service-based companies had to confront the daily challenges of managing people, material, marketing and delivery of the products. The distinction between two types of shares subsided, and with it, so did the separation between tangible and intangible qualities.

INDIVIDUALIZED FUTURITY:
PEOPLE AS ASSETS

The idea that businesses could be valued against their anticipated earnings released American capitalism from the slow-
paced economy of the past. By the late nineteenth century the
rate of growth of the US economy was twice, even three times,
anything that had been seen before. The next stage in the development of capitalism of futurity would begin after the Second
World War. At this point the economy of the future would learn
to incorporate individuals into its realm as well.

The process followed a similar type of logic. As more and
more people were employed by large enterprises or the government, jobs became better secured, often for life. Just like going
concerns in the corporate world, those salaried individuals in
secure jobs could now be treated as generating future income
streams continually. Credit in the form of mortgages, car loans
or plastic money could be advanced against those anticipated
future income streams. With the extension of credit, individuals simply followed what states and corporations had done ever
since the modern state system began to take shape, from around
the twelfth century: that is, they took on debt.

If centuries ago the banks grew rich by financing kings and
princes, now the banks grew rich by financing companies and
individuals. In a space of a few decades entire societies were financialized. By the late 1940s to early 1950s American capitalism
was defined not only by private ownership and free enterprise
but also by access to credit – first and foremost, mortgages: a
long-term loan to purchase a home.

Inevitably, the rise of the economy of futurity became a story of rising societal debt. Credit was not *allocated*, but generated across the economy, against future incomes. A system based on the massive growth in loans to states, firms and individuals, secured against future income streams, started to evolve. At its core, the process appears to be highly precarious: debts remained debts, and debt has to be repaid. Two issues would soon arise.

First, if everyone was busy borrowing, who is going to pay back the debt? Second, and related, if everyone was borrowing against anticipated future earnings, what happens if the future proved not as rosy as anticipated? The answer to the second question proved painfully simple: when the future turns sour, and people begin defaulting not only on capital repayment but also on interest payment, economies enter a crisis. The spectre of the financial system of the late twentieth and twenty-first centuries is a cycle of exuberance that inevitably ends with a financial crisis.

The link between futurity, exuberance and crisis is undoubtedly fascinating. In this book we are more interested, however, in the first question because it goes to the very heart of the modern mechanism of sabotage in the financial system. If everyone borrows against the future, who is paying back the debts accrued? The broad answer is: everyone. The specific answer depends on your position in the system. Within the infrastructure of the financial system, debt is recycled: someone buys the debts to ensure that the economy continues to function. Different types of individual debts are aggregated into investable securities and become assets that are purchased by investors. The hierarchy of debt repayments, in turn, reflects the hierarchy of the credit system itself: some debts must be paid back by the sale or acquisition of assets or collateral; some get written off; some are sold off to those willing to buy them, and some – especially if you are a big and important financial institution – can be monetized by a bailout from the state.

The alchemy of finance turned the famous saying of the Queen of Hearts in *Alice in Wonderland* into painful reality. In the modern world of finance we must run as fast as we can, just to stay in place. What we really need from the financiers, as Will Emerson put it in his inimitable language, is to keep their fingers on the scale: to make sure that we run as fast as we can simply to stay where we are; and if we want to go places, to grow, then we need to run twice as hard. There is a term for it in finance: it is called financial innovation, and we discuss this in the next chapter.

THE CYCLE OF LIFE AND DEBT

Let us take the example of the booming housing markets. People naturally want to own their homes. Most can afford it only by taking a mortgage. The financial sector can satisfy this demand for housing mortgages for a number of related reasons. First, governments encouraged and nurtured the demand for housing credit. This created a market for house borrowers and helped lower the cost of credit.[13] Second, bankers learned to assess risk profiles of individual borrowers, and this exercise has grown into an industry itself. Third, and that had become a crucial development in recent decades, banks were able to widen their mortgage offering tremendously by securitizing those mortgages. Risks associated with individual mortgages were bundled off into separate products and sold to third-party investors. These bundled products, an evolution on the old trading and agriculture futures, are known as mortgage-backed securities, or MBSs.

It is difficult to overstate the impact of the innovation of the MBS. On the one hand, MBS allowed banks to increase their mortgage offerings. They could do so by selling off these bundled securities to investors, freeing up capital for other types of lending. On the other, the flow of mortgage finance had the systemic effect of creating greater demand in the market (as housing stock could not grow as fast), leading to growth in asset prices.

It was a win-win situation, or so it appeared, as by and large borrowers saw the value of their major asset – the house – rise. Today, in most advanced capitalist countries, bar Germany and Switzerland, home ownership rates are above 60–70 per cent. Across many emerging markets, the ongoing rise of the middle classes is marked first and foremost by increased share of home ownership. On average, most people can afford to own a house only because a financial instrument that enables such ownership – a mortgage – is available. The bog-standard, twenty-five- or thirty-year prime mortgage remains the most important financial innovation politically, and not only in Anglo-Saxon economies.[14] Whether we realize it or not, we all are deeply invested in the normal functioning of the financial system and capital markets.

There are many political consequences to this relationship, and they are seldom understood. Most eloquent critiques of finance today tend to focus on the supply (or sell) side of this power game. They talk about risks identified and traded by financial markets that feed speculative bubbles; about financiers exploiting asymmetries of international regulation and scarce knowledge about financial products; about the power of the financial lobby to effect political outcomes in many parts of the world. There is a great degree of truth to these analyses. Often, however, the demand for financial products, or the buy side, either is assumed to be given or, more often, tends to be dismissed or overlooked.[15] And yet it is the demand side for financial products, and, more accurately, changes in the demand side, that has been one of the most influential forces driving changes in finance over the past few decades.

A whole set of factors, often unseen and rarely discussed, feeds the economy's and society's demand for credit and therefore debt. Changing demographics is probably the most important force creating an insatiable demand for financial products. People living longer and getting richer have boosted the demand for wealth to be managed professionally. As states have retreated from universal provision of welfare, even low- to mid-income households have become less reliant on bank finance and more keen to secure their financial future by using a variety of financial products. Correspondingly, there has been a sharp rise in the ratio of global wealth to income. Among Western economies, this ratio has roughly doubled since 1950 from around 200–300 per cent of GDP to around 400–600 per cent of GDP.[16]

The impact of this new demographics was summed up by the Bank of England's chief economist, Andy Haldane, in 2014. Globally, he noted, there are about $87tn of assets being professionally managed. Even on its own, it is a very large figure. It is equal to approximately one year's global GDP or around three quarters of the assets of the global banking industry.[17] More strikingly perhaps, since 1946, 'assets under management' (AUM) – that is, financialized wealth – have grown almost fivefold. Anglo-Saxon countries took the lead in the process, but the trend is similar across most OECD countries and many emerging markets.[18]

Other shifts boosted the demand side for debt-based financial products. During the twentieth century in OECD countries, states introduced mandatory pensions and mandatory insurances, such as car insurance. Mortgages are also often accompanied by life insurance or house insurance. The companies that manage these pension and insurance products – institutional investors – have a duty to invest their funds somewhere. Although the majority of these funds do not seek high-risk securities, they are nonetheless on an endless quest for interest-bearing financial assets. Institutional investors buy the securities generated through financial innovation, and products such as MBSs are traditionally considered to be high-quality investables.

The effects of these changes in demand were twofold. On the one hand, the growing demand for housing drove up mortgage offerings; rising prices of housing stock spurred the demand for house ownership further. On the other hand, an insatiable demand by investors for MBSs fuelled the market. From a household perspective a mortgage is a debt, and as more households took on increasing amounts of debt, regulators began to worry about the sustainability of the debt economy. But for investors such as pension funds, these 'debts' are 'assets'. Packaged as income-yielding securities, they are precisely what is needed to meet the demands of their balance sheets and store the value of savings their customers – you and us – entrust to them.

As societies grow older, and as more savings are being managed professionally, institutional investors need more and more of these assets. And so a new set of conditions began to characterize modern finance. The expanding market for MBSs provided households with greater opportunities to buy homes, making those homes more expensive in the process. Markets have become interlocked so that, overall, the pension funds, and indirectly their clients – the would-be pensioners – now have a great vested interest in the continuing growth of the mortgage market. Ostensibly, it is a win-win situation. (If we take a benign view of what had happened.)

We All Are in It Together

We can follow the same logic and apply it to industrial investment: a company needs to borrow funds to produce goods. The
company borrows against future income streams (by taking a
loan or issuing bonds or shares). The company employs workers
and invests the money in R&D, production and marketing. The
employees are forced to save some of their income in the form
of pensions and insurance. Pension funds and insurance companies buy debt instruments, including the debt the company
raised in order to produce the goods, as well as MBSs and the

FIGURE 2.1.

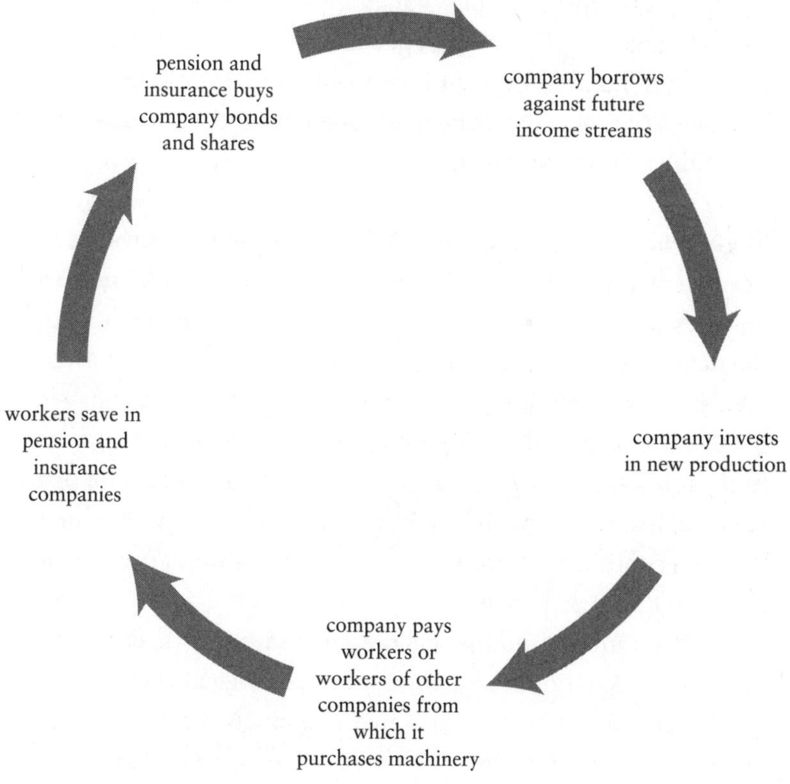

pension and
insurance buys
company bonds
and shares

company borrows
against future
income streams

company invests
in new production

workers save in
pension and
insurance
companies

company pays
workers or
workers of other
companies from
which it
purchases machinery

like. The company can thus borrow more funds, and the cycle goes on.

A system of interlocking markets evolved, most of which are complex, some truly esoteric. Their cumulative function is to sustain the type of consumerism and living standards we enjoy, just as Will Emerson explained so colourfully to his young colleague. Modern society works as long as these interlocking cycles of debt-instruments-turned-assets continue. But those interlocking markets can only work with the help of the financial system, with the fingers of Will Emerson 'on the scales'. Will and his colleagues in the banking sector need to advance credit to companies against their future income so that those companies can invest in new products and pay their workers. Will's counterparties in fund management invest workers' pension funds and insurance policies, storing people's long-term futures in financial investables. Or in our debts.

Modern finance does not only intermediate between savers and borrowers. It plays a crucial role in creating the capital needed for investment and ensuring that the credit is turned into assets, the demand for which seems to be insatiable. Since credit is not allocated but generated against futures, a highly sophisticated, if delicately balanced, economic system has emerged. It appears to be at least one size bigger than it should be: always running ahead of itself, speculating against futures that may never come. It is an economy that critics often describe as unreal, artificial, fictitious and even parasitic.

Paul Samuelson addressed the enigma of the economy of futurity. Consideration of a few simple and logical cases, he argued, 'raises doubt that there is anything much in celestial a priori reasoning from the axiom that what can be perceived about the future must already be "discounted" in current price quotations'.[19] Samuelson is correct. Logic and mathematics do not sustain an argument for futurity: borrowing on an unforeseeable future can move in any direction. It can easily turn sour, as it did in 2007–8, in 2000–2001, in 1997–98, in 1994, 1987, 1982, 1971–3 and in any of the financial crises that recurred throughout the twentieth century and long before. When the mood turns sour, we are collectively in deficit against the future. Many of the presumed 'assets' get revealed for what they are: defaulted debts. Money evaporates double quickly: one estimate suggests that about $50tn of global 'wealth' simply disappeared from the market during the 2007–9 financial crisis.[20]

It appears, therefore, that we inhabit an economy that logically does not make a great deal of sense. We have come to rely on the future for current consumption. The harsh reality is that there are no guarantees the future will be better than now. We rely on people like Will Emerson to take one-way 'bets' about this unforeseeable future on our behalf. But in a competitive market the Will Emersons are unlikely to make much money at all. Why should they have their 'fingers on the scale' in our favour? How can they possibly ensure that we enjoy this consumerist, oversized economy, when the market odds are struck against them?

Something had to give. And something did. A Faustian bargain was struck. Will and his colleagues *will* do their little magic and make money on it. But, doing so, they cannot play it 'fair' and by the rules of the market. Collectively, they need to do exactly what Veblen observed more than a hundred years ago: they make money by sabotaging their clients, their competitors, their governments and, ultimately, the market itself.

3

BE FIRST, BE SMARTER
AND CHEAT

Sabotage by Financial Innovation

Another character from the movie *Margin Call*, John Tuld, beautifully played by Jeremy Irons and based apparently on a composite of the real-life personalities of John Thain of Merrill Lynch and Lehman's Dick Fuld, lectures his board at a critical point of reckoning for his bank: 'There are three ways to make a living in this business...Be first, be smarter or cheat.'[1] But what if you don't have to choose between the three ways? A combination of the three tactics, according to John Tuld, would probably constitute the Holy Grail of truly big money in finance. Alas, it appears that such a Holy Grail does exist, and it is linked to the phenomenon of financial innovation.

'Innovation' has a nice ring to it. 'New' is probably the most popular word in advertising campaigns. Innovation has long defined human progress. The innovation of the internal-combustion engine changed human life beyond recognition. So did the innovation of the personal computer and the smartphone, and most medical innovations. We know comparatively little about financial innovation: in fact, there is only a thin academic literature on the concept, with most studies published after 2009. A wide definition comes from the regulators, who describe financial innovation as the introduction of 'something new that reduces costs, reduces risks or provides an improved product/service/instrument that better satisfies participants' demands' within a financial system.[2]

Who can object to that? What could possibly be wrong with improving services to clients? Alas, somehow innovation, at least in finance, often leaves a bitter aftertaste, not least among the many who have been sabotaged by the 'innovation'. One sceptic recently described financial innovation as, simply, regulatory arbitrage.[3] Or, put differently, a technique for sabotaging the public welfare and the government. We agree. Only we would add that if we have learned anything in the past four decades, it is that financial innovation includes the sabotage not only of governments but also of clients and competitors. It is this unique ability to combine all three of the qualities John Tuld lists to his board that seems to ensure really big money.

THE KING OF JUNK

In the early 1980s a certain Michael Milken invented what became known as the 'junk bond'; or, more elegantly, the high-yield bond. Junk bonds are considered among the most important innovations in twentieth-century finance. Their creator, Michael

Milken, would be widely celebrated by the industry. Eventually Milken's efforts would afford him residency of an exclusive gated community in California, better known as the Bay Area Prison.

On the surface, Milken's idea appeared innocuous enough. He spotted an opportunity which would enable companies with low credit ratings to borrow in the markets. Up to that point, such companies were not considered good borrowers and could thus raise money only very expensively. Milken set off to change minds by working with companies that for one reason or another had lost their credit ratings. He was convinced that those 'fallen angels' could be better managed and financed by a more innovative, 'structured' approach. The beauty of his idea was that these companies' low ratings meant they paid much higher interest on their bonds. Traditionally, high yield is a corollary of high risk. But in this case, risks could be reduced through better management of the companies. As a result, investors would get high-yield bonds with relatively low, managed risk. Put differently, companies that would receive the Milken treatment would attract new investment as their bonds would be snapped up in the market and could then use the money to improve their performance. A true win-win for all.

Working at Drexel Benham Lambert – the institution, now defunct, which had agreed to underwrite the enterprise – Milken created and dominated the over-the-counter (OTC) market in the new type of securities. OTC deals are exclusive, privately negotiated, one-off deals. These are not conducted on organized platforms and are only loosely regulated. Regulatory opacity in such markets allowed Milken to 'skirt the regulations'. Drexel provided the institutional background, including 'highly confident letters' related to the deals. The letter was a made-up document which had no legal standing in the market, but it looked solid enough to convince Milken's clients to part with their money embarking on new junk bond ventures.

Through Milken's initiative, Drexel became the salvation for many poorly rated companies which would not get financing otherwise. Drexel charged 3–4 per cent for their service, which was above the normal 1 per cent fee charged in established bond markets. Drexel's bankers also often demanded equity warrants for themselves and their buyers to sweeten the deal.[4] Junk bonds would certainly prove lucrative to Drexel. Reportedly the firm gloried in undercutting rivals and in stealing business from under the noses of a Wall Street elite which it viewed as snooty and indolent.

The business thrived. But Milken was not content to restrict himself to fallen angels. Soon he expanded and began to use junk bonds to finance leveraged buyouts of companies. 'Leveraged buyouts' (LBOs) is a polite term for corporate raiding. Junk bonds were used to finance the hugely ambitious corporate raiders and private equity firms.[5] Through junk bond leverage buyouts, companies with poor ratings could acquire better-performing companies. In the deal the acquiring company would use the target companies' funds to repay the debt it incurred to fund the takeover in the first place – ideally to Milken's bank. Junk bonds became the weapon of choice of hostile raiders churning up and destroying companies in the process. A junk-financed buyout of a company would bring on job losses and restructuring.[6] Gordon Gekko, the charismatic and ruthless character played by Michael Douglas in the movie *Wall Street*, is 'part Milken', according to one of the film's producers.

Drexel's ability to swiftly raise vast sums for LBOs was lucrative. By 1986 Drexel was Wall Street's most profitable firm and Milken its highest-paid executive: in 1986 the bank paid Milken nearly $295m ($665m in today's money), the next year he was paid $550m (or more than $1.2bn today).[7] But Drexel was feared and even loathed on Wall Street. 'Junk bonds, junk people,' was the typical sneer.[8]

Junk bonds could be used for a variety of purposes. But because of their relative novelty and the monopoly in the markets that Milken achieved so rapidly, the temptation to use them as a tool of sabotage was just too strong to resist. The reason appears trivial: money, greed, vanity.

In the early days of the twentieth-century US stock market it was the J. P. Morgans and the Rockefellers who dominated the market and developed an intimate knowledge of markets and clients. They used it as a powerful tool of sabotage: the bankers would literally force companies to join US Steel and set up trusts that controlled the market. In the 1980s Milken's intimate knowledge of the junk bond market and his clients gave him an enormous advantage, which he employed in a similar manner. The thin line between the two sides of the expanding business, that of the market maker and the market user, would eventually prove fatal to both Milken and Drexel. Armed with intimate information on clients and markets, Milken not only controlled the junk bond industry but also began to speculate on the prices of stocks and other securities. The temptation to use his inner market knowledge for insider trading appeared irresistible.

In 1989, a criminal investigation into Milken's affairs would find that he supplied Ivan Boesky – a trader with a history of convictions in insider trading – with both capital and information. The dealings culminated in stock market manipulation. The court found that Milken conspired with Boesky to inflate the price of a stock to benefit one of Drexel's clients. Similar trades were conducted with the agreement of other traders.

Notwithstanding their starring role as tools of sabotage, junk bonds outlived Milken. They remain an important funding instrument and a great source of profits for the industry. Financial institutions still charge a 3 per cent fee on junk bonds. Since 2005, the market – for both new and existing issues – has tripled and now totals some $2.2tn. In 2016 nearly $237bn of new high-yield securities were issued in the US.[9]

LEWIE RANIERI, MBS AND SECURITIZATION[10]

Just as Michael Milken was turning himself into a 'king of junk', another legendary character, Lewie Ranieri, a bright visionary at Salomon Brothers, spotted an opportunity in the bond business. At the time, the US bond market was dominated by government bonds. Ranieri is credited with turning the stale mortgage market into a vibrant bond-trading business, an innovation that would transform the industry and would eventually emerge as key contributor to the 2007–9 financial crisis.

Home mortgages, particularly the typical thirty-year fixed-rate American mortgages, are seen as nearly as secure as Treasury bonds (T-bonds). These securities could provide the type of steady monthly income that many institutional investors such as pension funds were after. Pension funds, however, would not purchase each mortgage separately. Their potential interest was in their aggregation, that is, in the financial products based on those mortgages. But the market for those standardized financial products faced a major hurdle: homebuyers could prepay the mortgages at any time. Most likely, they would have done so at a time when interest rates were low, just when investors had few alternative investment opportunities. Consequently, investors have tended to shy away from the mortgage-backed bonds.

Ranieri had the instinct and a strategy to change the parameters of the industry. Having put together a team that included some excellent mathematicians, he was able to optimize the risk of prepayment by slicing those thirty-year mortgages into five-to ten-year mortgage-backed securities. Coincidentally, the interest rate hike of Paul Volcker, as well as a change in taxation, helped spur the supply of mortgages from thrifts, which sought to sell their mortgages during those days of high interest rates. In a volatile market, Ranieri's desk was just about the only buyer of those mortgages. In parallel, Ranieri and his team lobbied policymakers in Washington for legislative changes that would make MBSs an authorized security across the country, aiming to add liquidity, scale and depth to the market he had been nurturing.

Just like in the case of Milken's junk bonds, the key to Ranieri's innovation was not only the product, the MBS, but the process of managing the associated risks. It would soon become known as securitization – the practice of converting illiquid assets such as mortgages into tradable securities through a set of legal fictions and financial engineering. Together, the new product and new techniques of securitization would change the banking system. The changes would receive a particular boost around 2001–2, long after Salomon was gone and just as 'democratization of credit', and specifically of the housing market, would become internationalized.

Armed with new techniques of securitization, banks would now actively originate new mortgages and remove them from their balance sheets by passing the risks on to investors. The fees for the sale of newly created securities to investors were a great incentive. Prizes were awarded for the most successful deals packaging poor-quality debts into ostensibly liquid securities. Credit-rating agencies became an integral cog in the machinery, having profited greatly from giving high ratings to securities underpinned by poor-quality loans. The new technique meant that banks, and their employees, now had new incentive schemes to sabotage both the clients, the borrowers and financial counterparties.

If one's bonus is dependent on the amount of loans one can generate, or on the ability to securitize those loans and sell them on, it is all too tempting to use all the imagination you have to generate precisely such outcomes. Banks, brokers, traders and investors enthusiastically embraced MBSs as a tool of sabotage, and the range of opportunities for securitization appeared limitless. Practically any financial asset, from car loans and student loans, to credit card receivables and MBSs themselves, would be securitized. And as loans were repackaged and resold as securities, the loan providers were looking for new borrowers to create yet more credit, which they could then pass on further into the securitization chain.

A massive credit boom was in the making, hailed as a new age of finance and the new era of 'great moderation'. Economists and policymakers would celebrate the achievements of the day, unimaginable only a decade before: low unemployment coincided with low inflation, all due to the great financial innovations of the day, supported by deregulation and democratization of credit. Every financial institution had a stake in the boom, with banks at centre stage. Sceptics were killjoys: socialists of one sort or another, eternal pessimists, or people who lived in the past and just did not get it.

The credit boom, combined with the opacity of most securitization deals, offered ample opportunities for profit making through sabotage. Mortgage brokers charged commissions, mortgage originators charged fees. Profits and bonuses were linked now to securitization products. The 'market' was geared towards finding any possible borrowers – homebuyers, car buyers, shoppers, tourists, students, viable and not – anyone who was prepared to sign on the dotted line. A whole segment of ultra-risky loans emerged, including so-called NINJA loans (loans to people with no income, no job and no assets). Fraud was common. Across the 'advanced industrialized world', documents were doctored and regulations skirted, as everyone wanted to participate in the boom.

Brokers offered homebuyers 'teaser rates', an appealingly low rate of interest on the mortgage which only lasted a few years in the very beginning of the deal. After that teaser period ended, the interest rates would shoot up, but the borrower had no opportunity to change either the policy or the product. It was all written in very fine print. Once the teaser period ended, many borrowers were unable to repay the interest on the loan, let alone the loan, and had to either sell their properties or face foreclosure.

The key to success in the loan securitization business was to get rid of them double quick. Sell them on, take commission, ensure that someone else is left holding the risk and start all over again. By the time those 'packaged securities' failed, which inevitably they did, someone else would pick up the tab. Business was good. Banks were so intent on selling securities to investors that many soon began to deliberately misrepresent the quality of the underlying loans. Just like in the Roaring Twenties, banks and investment funds simply forgot their fiduciary duties. According to one estimate, the misrepresentations concerned mortgages with a combined outstanding balance of up to $160bn, while the underwriters may be liable for about $60bn in representation and warranty damages.[11] The estimate is likely to be conservative.

As the credit boom escalated, more banks developed the habit of misrepresenting the true nature of the mortgages underpinning the bonds they were offering. Some remained cautious; a few were aware of the fraud. But as Chuck Prince, Citigroup's CEO, famously explained, 'You need to dance as long as the music was playing.' A bank that failed to 'compete' with the rest in finding ever more dodgy borrowers, and selling those securities on, would lose 'talent', reputation and capital.

In the summer of 2007, the music did stop. The world's premier banks would face a multitude of charges, many of them criminal, for mortgage, wire, postal and securities fraud. At Bank of America and its subsidiaries, 'it has been shown repeatedly that the origination process…failed to live up to their own internal guidelines and the resulting loans did not reflect the way they were characterized to investors.'[12] Many institutions settled out of court for misrepresentations in their securitization processes. In 2018, a decade after the crisis, Barclays agreed to a $2bn settlement with the US justice department over the sale of MBSs in the lead-up to the 2008 crisis. Two former Barclays executives have settled for $2m.[13]

The management of another bank that stars in this book, RBS, was accused by US authorities of misrepresenting 'material facts to deceive and cheat its customers in trades', in a variety of ways. RBS traders would lie to buyers about a seller's asking price; in other instances they invented a fictitious third-party seller to charge the buyer an extra commission. Deirdre Daly, US attorney for Connecticut, noted: 'For years, RBS fostered a culture of securities fraud. Those in a position of authority taught and encouraged fraudulent trading practices…Worse, those supervisors and compliance personnel then took steps to prevent victims and honest RBS employees from discovering and exposing the scheme.' RBS settled out of court.[14]

Overall, banks on both sides of the Atlantic have paid \$321bn in fines for misrepresentation to customers and investors, with Bank of America and J. P. Morgan Chase paying the largest amounts. North American banks accounted for nearly 63 per cent of the total fines.[15] Millions of Americans lost their homes, while the legacy of the 2007–9 crisis lives on in today's politics on both sides of the Atlantic.

It can be, and has been, argued that, in itself, securitization is not a tool of sabotage. But in the reality of innovation, competition and opacity it did become one. In 2009 Ranieri would confess: 'I do feel guilty…I wasn't out to invent the biggest floating craps game of all time, but that's what happened…These are real people losing their homes. I feel a responsibility for dealing with it in a way that's up close and personal.'[16] Both the MBSs and securitization remain important institutional features of today's finance. In 2017 the volume of MBSs in the US bond market alone was just over \$9tn, the second-largest segment of the bond market after US Treasuries.[17] MBSs continue to be widely recognized as safe investables by institutions around the world. Securitization, too, remains standard practice in the financial industry, with the European Union actively encouraging the creation of the European capital market, with 'high quality and liquid' securitization deemed its main driver.

Be First, Be Smarter and Cheat

BLYTHE MASTERS AND THE CDS[18]

Shortly after the revolutions launched by Milken and Ranieri, another visionary in another legendary institution would come across another opportunity. Blythe Masters and her team at J. P. Morgan would create and finesse a product which would spur the credit boom of 2002–7 and, employed as a weapon of sabotage, eventually precipitate its implosion.

Traditionally, banks made money by issuing loans to the corporate sector. The problem, however, was that because of the risk of default of the borrowers, banks were required to hold on to capital as a reserve, to hedge against that risk. If only banks could find a way to get rid of the risk of a default by a corporate client! This would free a lot of capital which could then be directed to other ventures and types of lending.

Masters' idea was ingenious and simple: why not insure the bank against those risks and pass them on to the insurer, thus freeing capital for other investment? Blythe Masters and her team at J. P. Morgan set off to seek such an insurer, and soon found one. American Insurance Group (AIG) was happy to provide such an insurance to J. P. Morgan, for a fee. The deal was formalized in a financial instrument which would later become known as a credit default swap (CDS). The formula devised at J. P. Morgan proved highly popular. Soon other banks and hedge funds joined the business of selling and buying the CDSs.

In the abstract world of economics, where a bank is a responsible intermediary, this invention was ingenious and effective. But in the real-life business of finance, with lack of regulations, tough competition and greed, the invention became a perfect tool of moneymaking through sabotage. Both by design and by application, the CDS would prove an ideal instrument of sabotage.

CDSs were devised and used as insurance instruments, designed to protect creditors against losses in case of default. Insurance products are based on the concept of insurable interest, traditionally are tightly regulated and require more capital. But when CDSs were being launched, no one wanted to get bogged down with insurance regulations. The solution was not to call those products insurance. Instead, the products were called swaps – a type of a financial derivative, traded on private, OTC markets and thus unregulated.[19]

Eventually, the technique was adapted by the industry to insure not only corporate default risk, but also risks of subprime mortgages and other low-quality loans. Soon banks and hedge funds realized they did not have to bother with actual bonds, but could simply trade CDSs. In fact it would soon prove much easier and quicker to buy and sell CDS contracts rather than buy and sell actual bonds. The beauty of the new market was that CDSs could now be bought and sold by firms that had no economic interest in the underlying entities.[20] A myriad of CDS-based derivatives were created and traded, with little or no assets underpinning them.

It is easy to see how an instrument devised to arrange a payout in case of a borrower's default could be used to ensure that the lender, or someone simply holding the CDS, benefits from the borrower's default. CDSs could easily be used to sabotage the interests of a company or its debt holders. For example, a hedge fund could hold $200m of a company's bonds but could buy swap protection against the company's default in the CDS market for, say, $500m worth of the company's debt.[21] That means that the hedge fund now had an active interest in the company's failure.

The hedge fund stands to profit more from its swap position than it would lose from the bonds. Some hedge funds became specialists in pushing such companies into liquidation, typically settling in an out-of-court restructuring. When the American autoparts company Delphi Corp defaulted in 2005, the value of notional swaps on the company amounted to about $30bn, fifteen times its $2bn in bonds.[22] By the end of 2007, CDSs had grown to more than $60tn in global business.[23] The rest, as they say, is history.

CDSs proved particularly toxic as they were sold to cover exotic financial instruments created during the subprime boom. As MBSs and collateralized debt obligations became nearly worthless, defaults were triggered across the system. The banks and hedge funds that were lured by easy fees, and had sold CDSs to others during the boom, now faced mounting costs. An element of the unknown added to the panic: as CDSs were traded over the counter, no one knew exactly the overall exposure to these products. In a quirk of financial complexity, it would turn out that in their great enthusiasm for these products many banks and hedge funds simultaneously bought and sold CDSs, and many were now lucky enough to 'nett out' their CDS positions.[24]

Not AIG, though. AIG only sold CDSs to others; it never bought them. Once bonds defaulted, AIG – the main insurer – had to pay out to many parties across the industry, but nobody was paying the AIG. The insurance giant was caught in a downward spiral of its own making, with defaults cascading down the structures. Notionally, CDSs written by AIG covered more than $440bn in bonds, money AIG simply did not have. AIG's credit rating was downgraded, with material consequences: the insurer now needed to put up more collateral to guarantee its ability to pay. The firm was not able to do that.[25] In September 2008 AIG was bailed out by the US government, via $85bn in loans for AIG in exchange for an 80 per cent stake in the company. The eventual financial help from the government to AIG would total $182bn.

The bailout of AIG can be easily interpreted as yet another case of a 'too big to fail' problem: the US government simply could not afford to let the insurance giant go down. But on Wall Street a more cynical theory was making the rounds at the time. 'The whole point of the bailout was to save Goldman Sachs,' said Christopher Whalen, head of financial advisory services for Institutional Risk Analytics. 'The...thing is so rancid and so hideous.' At the time, a Goldman Sachs spokesman declined to comment on the AIG bailout or what government funds it received. Weeks later AIG told investors that 'the vast majority' of taxpayer funds were simply 'passed through AIG to other financial institutions' as it unwound transactions. Between September and December 2008 more than $50bn of payments went to counterparty banks. Goldman and Deutsche Bank AG were the largest trading parties, each receiving about $6bn.[26]

Could the original team at J. P. Morgan have envisaged the fall of their main insurer and a system-wide application of the security as tool of sabotage? Even in the wake of the crisis Blythe Masters would continue to defend her innovation, admitting nonetheless that 'tools that transfer risk can also increase systemic risk if major counterparties fail to manage their exposures properly'.[27] But clearly both in the design of the security itself – misnamed as a derivative – and in the way it was adopted by the market, the CDSs were used extensively to sabotage parties by allowing the banks to gamble on companies' failure. The instruments enabled many banks to shield themselves from losses, at the expense of investors. Ultimately, CDSs became a tool of the sabotage of government as well, entrapping a giant insurer on one side of the CDS business.

THE BITTER AFTERTASTE OF FINANCIAL INNOVATION

A classic scholar of business behaviour, Joseph Schumpeter, saw innovation as an important source of market power.[28] Schumpeter analysed various innovations: the introduction of new products, new methods of production and new forms of business organization, as well as the penetration of new markets. Crucially, he argued, it is not a mere invention or a new product, or even several such products, that transforms an economy, but 'the carrying out of new combinations' that works as the key driver of economic change.[29]

Michael Milken, Lewie Ranieri and Blythe Masters became celebrities in the world of finance and beyond. Their names feature in financial bestsellers and popular culture. But rarely is it the individual financier who generates meaningful change. Milken, Ranieri and Masters each had teams of professionals working with them and, more importantly, powerful financial institutions supporting their market-making efforts. Just as Schumpeter noted, it was the combination of innovations in products and techniques and the institutionalization of a new market that created a lasting legacy for the industry, precipitated economic change and, as John Tuld remarks, was a sure a way to make money in the business of finance.

In finance, however, aggregation always poses a problem. Even if at the individual level innovations can bring cost improvements and benefits, at the level of the system these benefits are uncertain. For individual economic agents, financial derivatives can be a great solution to managing risks. For the system as a whole, financial derivatives can easily turn into 'weapons of mass destruction' because they often amplify the risks and costs in unpredictable ways. Junk bonds, MBSs, securitization and CDSs were adopted so enthusiastically by the 'market' because they could be used as instruments of sabotage.

Commonly known as the paradox of aggregation,[30] the phenomenon has many facets, with a direct implication for our understanding of the role of financial innovation. First, new financial products and processes tend to be shrouded in complexity, meaning that the full spectrum of information about them may never be available to buyer, client or the regulator.[31] Second, always and everywhere, financial innovations are transactions in futurity. This means that buyers often discover an unwanted or risky element far too late, and it may be impossible to correct the outcome due to the conditions of the contract. Third, financial innovations increasingly span several markets, making oversight and regulation of the process extremely challenging. Historically, regulatory arbitrage has been feeding a lot of financial and legal innovation.

These three elements, we argue, make financial innovation not only the ideal tactic of moneymaking but also a perfect tool in the Veblenian arsenal of sabotage. As an industry, finance is uniquely primed to capitalize on the opportunity to carry out such 'new combinations'. By innovating new types of financial assets – often by combining several aspects of economic activity in a new way and creating a market for this practice – financial innovators gain a structural advance over others in the industry, the regulators and society. Indeed, the experience of junk bonds, securitization or credit derivatives suggests that it is never the invention of a specific financial product that endows the innovator with a degree of power and profit, but the wider institutionalization of this product in the infrastructure of the new market, a regulatory niche and an accommodating political-economic system. And that is something, we believe, regulators should begin to take on board.

As this book goes to press, economies around the world are gripped by the advance of artificial intelligence (AI) and a spate of new financial technologies. The emergence of data as the most valuable asset in the digital capitalism of the twenty-first century, as well as tighter regulation of the traditional financial sector, is paving the way for a new means of doing the business of finance.

Many of these innovations are celebrated in the market and beyond. Blockchain – a distributed ledger technology underpinning the drive – is heralded as the radically new way to connect people across various sectors and walks of life. It is rapidly transforming the way business is conducted and services are delivered, from the energy sector to adult entertainers, as well as public services such as insurance and healthcare. Blockchain is probably best compared to the financial equivalent of the invention of email, a seemingly isolated revolution in communication which back in the mid-1990s would herald the rise of a new type of economic organization.

Enthusiasts argue that a blockchain-powered economy can overcome a lot of the ills and costs of the traditional ways of doing business in finance.

Currently, we rely on a dated financial system that depends on paper and outdated software. It is expensive and completely open to fraud and crime. Blockchain disrupts the current bank system by being a real-time updating digital ledger that cannot be changed. This takes paper and fraud out of the equation. Wire and transfer fees will be decreased by using bitcoin, clearing and settlement can happen instantly, loans and credit applications can be assessed on the spot and consumers will have instant access to the funds they need and the answers they require.[32]

The political appeal of blockchain is rather unique. The Right cheers the ability of the technology to force a decentralization of the system and independence from formal governance structures. The Left sees an enormous potential of blockchain to democratize finance as a system that has become systemically corrupt, and thus empower people's direct participation. Academics and economic historians are convinced that technology will forever change banking as we know it.

Veblenians are among those who do not share the general enthusiasm. They cast a weary eye on blockchain and its offspring, as well as on the whole new fintech phenomenon.

For a good reason.

PART TWO

'NO CONFLICT, NO INTEREST'

Sabotaging the Clients

Finance had become a central, even structural dimension of modern life. Everyone in the modern world – individuals, households, small or large businesses, public bodies – relies on finance for even the most mundane of economic affairs. Everyone must have an account with a bank. Everyone is, therefore, a client of a bank. Theoretically, reliance on banks should be lucrative enough. We pay monthly or annual fees to banks for maintaining our accounts; we pay fees for overdrafts and interest on loans. Our deposits, so the theory holds, can be used by banks for further lending. The banks can live comfortably as retail banking. But is this enough? Not really. Our reliance on banks is also an opportunity for those banks to sabotage us, the clients, with the simple aim of generating extra profits.

SABOTAGE

Sabotaging clients, whether those clients are individuals, small companies, or other banks and other financial institutions, involves, as we will see, taking advantage of private information about the client's intention and/or exploiting their credulity and lack of expertise. There are other opportunities too. It can be giving advice to clients: offering 'tips' to buy certain products which the bank believes will perform poorly. The bank charges hefty commission for the bad advice. The bank can then hedge against the very advice to clients, fleecing them of additional funds. Banks have become rather innovative and sophisticated in doing so, taking advantage of a client's lack of knowledge of derivatives and swap arrangements. The client's losses end up as the bank's gains, and the commission on the bad advice is only the cherry on the cake – the cake being the bank's profits and the adviser's bonuses.

Another strategy is for a brokerage entity to take advantage of knowing the client's ask price (on shares, derivatives or foreign currencies) and then to pocket the difference, while charging brokerage fees. A client – say, a pension fund – puts a large order with a broker to purchase, for instance, Apple's shares. The pension fund puts an upper limit on the ask price it is prepared to pay for those shares. The broker can use their own funds, or can borrow funds to purchase a large quantity of Apple shares, and the moment those shares reach the upper ask price of their client, the broker sells the shares they bought to the client, at the upper ask price, and with a tidy profit.

With changes spurred by new technologies, the practice is not only institutionalized but also automated. The spread of algorithmic trading has enabled big firms like Citadel or Gekko to 'front-run' asset managers' orders. Their profits come from two sources of privileged access. On the one hand, they know the price their client is prepared to pay for a security. On the other, they know or, in the case of so-called dark pools, control the current market for that security, and can profit from a nanosecond advantage of 'front-running' the client's order, thus manipulating the overall price level in the market.

Stories of such a nature abound. Below we recall a select few of the harrowing cases that made the headlines both during and after the financial crisis, focusing on behaviour at the Royal Bank of Scotland (RBS) in the UK, and at Goldman Sachs and Wells Fargo in US.

4

—

DEAD SOULS AT THE ROYAL
BANK OF SCOTLAND

'But they are *dead* souls,' replies Nastasia Petrovna, a provincial landowner, to Chichikov, an aspiring nobleman, who offers to buy the lists of dead peasants that used to belong to her.

'Who said they were not? The mere fact of their being dead entails upon you a loss as dead as the souls, for you have to continue paying tax upon them, whereas *my* plan is to relieve you both of the tax and of the resultant trouble...'

'Yes – though I do not know...You see, never before have I sold dead souls.'

'Quite so. It would be a surprising thing if you had. But surely you do not think that these dead souls are in the least worth keeping?'

'Oh, no, indeed! Why should they be worth keeping? I am sure they are not so. The only thing which troubles me is the fact that they are...*dead*.'

Nikolai Gogol, *Dead Souls*, 1842

Nastasia Petrovna would not make a manager at RBS. There, dead souls were for keeps. During the boom years, upon receiving the news of a customer's death, account managers would quickly upgrade the accounts of newly deceased customers to Premier accounts, for a bonus, and only then file the death certificates. Later this would be classified as a small-scale scam.[1]

RBS staff were no match for Gogol's Chichikov: dead souls were his only business venture. At RBS, using deceased clients was only one of the many areas of business. Staff simply used the accounts of the deceased customers to add to their bonuses by exploiting time and reporting gaps. It was one of many routes to bonuses, penalty-free: there was no chance that the newly deceased customers would actually make noise about their new expensive Premier accounts.

Forgery was another. 'It was common knowledge that all the best business was done at the photocopier and Broadland business park,' an RBS whistleblower told a UK Parliamentary Select Committee. The 'business' in question refers to forging customers' signatures on loan agreements and guarantees provided by the bank. It transpired that during their induction RBS staff were given specific training on handling unsigned documentation required for a transaction with the bank. There were four steps to follow:

1. Extract the customer's signature from the Individual Signature Verification (ISV) section of the customer's central file records.

2. Take a copy of the document where the signature was missing and then place it over the version from the ISV system against a window. With the light shining through the original, the signature could then be traced (forged) onto the necessary document.
3. Obscure the image. The document should be run through the photocopier several times, including some slightly out-of-line versions, altering the density settings.
4. Scan the photocopied version into the system.

The idea was to ensure that the original 'wet ink' version of the forged document would never be available on file for ink date testing in case of a dispute.[2] The loan agreements and guarantees, in turn, often were processed without the customer's knowledge. The overall aim of these exercises, a UK Parliamentary Committee would discover, was to pass on to customers as much of RBS's bad debts as possible, while at the same time to extract 'value' from small- and medium-size business customers to buffer the bank's profits.

There hardly appears to be any aspect of business at RBS that was *not* sabotage. Following the onset of the financial-market contagion from the subprime debt crisis, the bank sought to off-load some of its ill-judged long-term interest rate swaps. Many of those deals, known as interest rate swaps, had been signed during the good times with the intention of protecting the bank against interest rate rises. Now that interest rates were tumbling, those swaps arrangements threatened to cost RBS billions upon billions of dollars. Managers at RBS (though, admittedly, not only at the RBS) hit on the ingenious idea that their own customers were their best bet of resolving this problem. The key to those solutions would lie in the financial planning and advice offered by the bank to its customers. The advice would prompt a nine-year-old daughter of one of RBS's customers to conclude: 'First rule of life: never trust a bank.'

Context is important here. In 2007 the bank's own economic forecasters concurred with the general prognosis (as confirmed by the bank's feeds on terminals) that interest rates were heading south, quite dramatically, and were due to remain so for a long time. RBS opted, instead, to urge its customers to purchase 'protection' against interest rate rises. Some of those unsuspecting clients would end up purchasing the bank's own high-fixed-rate deals, helping the bank to clear some of its potential liabilities. To help with the deal, RBS would often loan their customers the funds necessary to buy the costly hedges, at fixed interest rates of 7 or 8 per cent – at a time when interest rates were heading towards 0 per cent, thus making extra profits. The scheme worked so smoothly (for RBS, not the clients) that thereafter, and separately, RBS required all members of the RBS Group to make all new commercial loans over £500k subject to the purchase of interest rate swaps. 'Every deal which we have seen sold to an RBS customer,' concluded the UK Parliamentary Committee, was a 'heads we win, tails you lose' trade: the customer was always the loser.[3]

A variety of schemes was used to incentivize staff. RBS business managers were given 'ovation' vouchers, tax free and acceptable as a payment method by major stores. A special 'reward' was given for introducing business customers to employees in the RBS Markets team, where such customers were subsequently sold those expensive hedging products. An RBS corporate manager could double his year's basic salary with additional bonuses by helping to sell only a few interest rate swaps to his customers.

Some single sales alone could be worth 20–30 per cent of an annual target.[4]

A whole division within RBS was dedicated to helping customers in difficulties: the Global Restructuring Group (GRG), so renamed in 2009 to oversee some 16,500 small and medium enterprises (SMEs) in distress with assets worth £65bn that had been placed in special measures.[5] GRG's mission was described by the law firm Clifford Chance, RBS's lawyers, as 'to return customers to financial health and to protect the bank's position by minimising losses and maximising recoveries'.[6] It was the latter and not the former that proved to be the case. One insight into the techniques used at GRG can be gleaned from an internal memo written in 2009 by a junior manager there. The memo contained guidance on how to manage the group's clients. It included the following: 'Rope: Sometimes you have to let customers hang themselves. You have then gained their trust and they know what's coming when they fail to deliver.' And further advice on fee setting: 'Avoid round number fees – £5,300 sounds as if you have thought about it, £5k sounds like you haven't.'[7]

GRG had a wide remit. It was able to unilaterally change the lending terms of original loans without notice or negotiation, by way of a blandly inconspicuous clause in RBS's standard loan agreement: 'the agreement replaces all previous agreements in relation to the loan'.[8] New terms would be imposed, including radically increased lending rates, combined with those unnecessary and expensive hedging agreements, and even what were known as 'Upside' instruments – property participation fee agreements (PPFAs) or equity participation agreements (EPAs). These ensured that GRG would receive, respectively, a percentage of the value of assets or free shares in the business.

In numerous cases, businesses were stripped of their remaining assets and forced into bankruptcy. There is evidence that at least some businesses were placed in special measures unnecessarily, forced in through minor breaches of covenants or revised loan-to-value ratios that deliberately understated the value of assets. The UK parliamentary committee concluded that GRG would often collude with other professionals to enrich themselves at the company's expense. The threat of clients taking legal action was minimized by RBS's ability to coerce or bribe legal practices into refusing to act for aggrieved SME owners.[9]

RBS customers were sent to GRG when undisclosed credit lines, often in the hundreds of thousands, or even millions, breached their loan-to-value loan covenants, without their knowledge. Those customers had no chance of surviving the GRG treatment.

RBS VS DAVID EASTER

One typical example of the GRG treatment is that of David Easter, a former corporate headhunter, who developed a hotel chain known as the Arlington Hotel Group with the aid of an RBS division, NatWest. It was a healthy business, with a turnover of nearly £5m per annum and buoyant profits, and Easter had hopes of building a chain of at least ten hotels in villages throughout East Anglia.

In December 2010 his bank manager informed Easter that the business was being transferred to GRG. To Easter, this came as a shock: 'I didn't understand why they were doing this to me. They were saying we had broken a covenant on our loan, but we had never missed a payment.'[10] GRG immediately began charging the

Arlington Hotel Group large fees. A 'review fee' of £400 a month was added to the bill, as was a 'risk fee' of £150,000 per year, and a £7,000 fee for 'security'. The interest rate on the original loan was increased to 3.5 per cent above the bank rate, instead of the original 1.25 per cent. Easter's problems with GRG escalated when the division conducted a revaluation of the business, to just £4.5m. This was considerably lower than the £6m figure provided by Easter's own valuation team, or the £5.2m estimate provided by another valuation firm. Peculiarly, it did not include one lucrative hotel in the chain. GRG now demanded that Easter pay the bank back almost £5m within a year, although the original loan had been extended for the longer period of fifteen years.

The extra payments began to undermine the health of the business. David Easter struggled to pay VAT and his suppliers, and was forced to request an overdraft facility of £40,000 to buy essential supplies, but this only brought an extra payment of £2,000, just for the privilege of having it. By 2012 Easter began selling hotels in the chain. The auditors PricewaterhouseCoopers, imposed on him by GRG, charged £10,000 per month, plus 3 per cent of the value of the hotels that were being sold. By 2013 the entire Arlington chain was put into liquidation, and was finally dissolved in April 2014. PWC provides a fourteen-page summary of the administration process for Arlington Place Hotels. Among other things, the document states that 'The Bank [RBS] has recovered £424,604 under its fixed charges security over the Company's assets. The Bank on appointment was owed £2.21m and so has suffered a significant shortfall on its lending.'[11] No further documentation related to David Easter's case is currently available in the public domain. The weblink to the Arlington Place Hotels case provided by PWC does not exist.

SABOTAGE

RBS VS DEREK CARLYLE

Mr Carlyle, a developer, had been a long-standing customer of RBS. He had an 'excellent working relationship' with the bank.[12] RBS had been happy to provide funding for Carlyle's successful developments. The profit margin on the projects was around 30 per cent, which made RBS a willing partner. In 2007 Carlyle had one active project, in East Kilbride, when land became available for development in Perthshire. It was attached to the prestigious Gleneagles Hotel.

Given the likely profit from the venture, Mr Carlyle proposed to RBS that they help fund the purchase and development of the land. In March 2007 he met a representative from the bank's commercial centre to discuss terms. The funding was to be advanced in two stages – the initial land purchase, and the development of a house, with a combined projected value of £4m. One of the conditions of the sale was a buy-back clause: Mr Carlyle could not resell the plot, and it must be developed within a year; otherwise, it would revert to the vendors. This clause had prompted Mr Carlyle to request that the funding from RBS must be made available for both purchase and development, without which the venture would not be worth pursuing.

Initially RBS agreed, as the project was a promising one. Given the consistency of his former dealings with RBS, and the bank's apparent enthusiasm, Mr Carlyle purchased the land, and the funding (£845,000 and £560,000) was finally released in August 2007. Although the development part of the funds was not provided, the bank continued to promise support, and Carlyle used his own money to begin building, and also used the sale of another property to repay some outstanding debts to the bank.

However, the bank suddenly changed its mind about the funding provision. On 12 August 2008 Mr Carlyle and his solicitors were informed that RBS required immediate repayment of the £1.45m that it had provided for the purchase. Money was to be paid by 10.30 a.m. the next day, 'or', it said, it would 'destroy' Mr Carlyle; it advised him that he 'should be clear about the chaos that would ensue' if he didn't pay.[13]

RBS justified its action by claiming that it had never agreed to the funding of the development, and that any funds that Carlyle had acquired through selling another property should have been paid immediately to the bank. RBS claimed that an agreement was in place to this effect, although no document has ever been produced to prove this.

RBS then began a series of actions designed to force Mr Carlyle to immediately pay the bank £1.45m. These included freezing Carlyle's bank accounts, forcing his company to shut down, taking over his assets, and issuing arrestment and inhibition orders from Edinburgh's Court of Session. He was put into sequestration (the term for personal bankruptcy in Scotland) despite having a portfolio of properties worth some £8m and personal debts of less than £5m.[14] In addition, the bank moved to possess Carlyle's family home.

RBS manoeuvred funds deposited in a personal bank account dedicated to the payment of Carlyle's children's school fees so that funds were drained from the account and the school fees went unpaid. It used its considerable influence with local firms of solicitors to frighten them into refusing to take Carlyle's case. The firm that finally accepted his brief, MBM Commercial, did so only after obtaining RBS's permission. To compound Mr Carlyle's situation, amid the unfolding crisis, the East Kilbride development project was sold for half its real value after being expropriated by the bank.

This catalogue of destruction and malice caused tremendous pain and stress to the entire family and severely impaired Carlyle's reputation. RBS, however, continued to harass Carlyle through the aegis of the Court of Sessions. When Carlyle counterclaimed that the bank had reneged on its promise to him, which amounted to a breach of contract, known as collateral warranty, the Court of Sessions found in favour of Carlyle and decided that RBS had in fact been in breach of its contract. Lord Glennie's judgment of 13 January 2010 supported Carlyle's claim that the bank's behaviour within the court had not met the required standards, and that RBS had displayed an absence of 'candour' during the case. Glennie also noted that 'the pleading of the Bank's case on this matter fell far below the standard which the court is entitled to expect'.[15]

The case of Mr Carlyle received some publicity. Speaking in Parliament on behalf of Mr Carlyle, Jim Hood, MP, explained that he had personally experienced RBS's duplicity, when he attempted to intercede on Carlyle's behalf by writing to Alan Dickinson, the chief executive of RBS. It appeared that Dickinson was given a distorted report of the proceedings against Carlyle by the branch of GRG in Edinburgh. Other instances of the bank's 'lack of candour' included an attempt to persuade the Court of Sessions, Alan Dickinson and Carlyle's solicitors that an RBS manager who was Carlyle's chief witness had changed her original statement that had supported Carlyle's claim that a breach of contract had taken place. This turned out to be false, as the RBS manager had never retracted her first statement. Beyond that, RBS also attempted to arrange for Carlyle to be sequestrated for owing another small-scale debt (£4,000) to another party. This debt had nothing to do with the RBS case, but it was a convenient opportunity for the bank to destroy Mr Carlyle's credibility with the court.

In 2013 RBS appealed against Lord Glennie's judgment. Three Scottish judges reversed the original verdict. In 2015 the verdict was unanimously reinstated by the Supreme Court. In 2016 RBS apologized for 'poor treatment of its customers' and agreed to compensate them to the tune of £400m.[16] In 2017 a settlement was finally reached with RBS, with the final terms being kept secret.[17]

There are many stories of this nature. Some business customers were being sold into known losses by RBS managers and their Markets team affiliates. As those losses increased when interest rates dropped, many had gone bust under liabilities that had never been declared to them. In his foreword to the Parliamentary report, the chair, Sir Callum McCarthy, notes that RBS took advantage of regulatory blind spots:

> Most of GRG's customer-facing activities, in common with all features of bank lending to SME customers, were not regulated by the Financial Standards Authority at the time…the impropriate actions we identify, and their wide-ranging consequences for customers, arose in areas which, with minor exceptions, were not subject to regulatory rules or principles. Accordingly, the scope for regulatory action is limited, and it seems court action by those affected is unlikely to be practicable.[18]

This had been the behaviour of a quasi-nationalized bank, saved by the taxpayers from insolvency. In 2007 RBS was the world's largest bank, with assets valued at just under $4tn.

A decade after the crisis things have moved on – though not necessarily in the right direction. Under increased regulatory pressure on banks' bonuses, some inventive staff have resorted to using clients, existing and non-existing, to sabotage their own institutions to hit targets.

Several whistleblowers from the troubled RBS and its subsidiary NatWest report that the drive to sell is higher than before 2007. Staff are under heavy pressure to ram loans and mortgages onto customers ahead of the relaunch of Williams & Glyn, one of the RBS offspring. Cases of mis-selling and tricking customers into products they do not need do continue, with the practice used to help bank staff meet their 'un-negotiated and non-discussed sales targets', according to one whistleblower. Sabotaging clients appears to have become entrenched in the culture of RBS: 'You have no idea how this culture is rabid, and I work in NatWest. Telephone preference rules are ignored – the practice breaches data protection but we are told it's an acceptable risk and they will just pay the fine if they get caught.'[19]

Maybe this helps explain why, despite its official commitment since 2014 to become the 'most trusted' bank in the country, RBS remains the 'least popular' bank in the UK.[20] In the summer of 2018, after a four-year investigation, the UK Financial Conduct Authority concluded that it could not take any action against RBS over GRG because commercial lending was unregulated.[21]

5

'OUR PEOPLE ARE OUR GREATEST ASSET'

Goldman's Abacus

For a giant like RBS operating in an unregulated area, it was easy to gain profits by sabotaging small businesses and retail clients. But what if you are a more sophisticated institution? Why restrict yourself to individual borrowers?

Let us take Goldman Sachs, a premier member of the world's banking elite which has a reputation for scale and foresight. A friend of ours who happens to be a high-net-worth individual had assets and estate managed by Goldman for some time. After one of her conversations with us about the nature of business in finance she decided to ask her personal bank manager at Goldman to explain what specifically she was being charged for. The manager remained evasive and repeatedly refused to explain the structure of the fees. Bewildered, she withdrew her business from Goldman and tried a few other big banks, encountering similar problems. She eventually settled on a smaller and less-known institution.

Admired for smartness and innovation, Goldman may not need clients like our friend. It can go after banks and other institutions to develop new lines of business on a different scale. Goldman's now well-known Abacus affair centred on a set of esoteric financial instruments known as synthetic collateral debt obligations (or CDOs). A very simplified explanation of what a synthetic CDO is was helpfully provided by Matt Levine of Bloomberg:

1. Some investors put money in a 'pot'.
2. The pot writes a credit default swap to an investment bank – in this case, Goldman Sachs Group Inc. – insuring Goldman against the risk of default of some mortgage bonds (called the 'reference portfolio').
3. Goldman pays premiums for the credit default swap, and those payments are passed along to the CDO investors.
4. If some of the reference mortgage bonds default, then the 'pot' pays some money to Goldman. This reduces the 'pot' (and the premiums that Goldman pays to the investors).
5. At the end of the trade, the investors get back whatever is left in the 'pot': that is, their initial investment minus however much the pot has paid out to Goldman under the swap to cover it for defaults on the reference mortgage bonds.

The whole scheme is nothing but a bet on the performance of the reference bonds. Neither the investors nor the pot ever *own* the reference bonds; their exposure to the bonds is synthetic: it comes exclusively from a derivative contract with Goldman.[1]

A specific CDO deal piqued the interest of the US Securities and Exchange Commission. The deal was arranged by Goldman on behalf of John Paulson, a fund manager. By 2006 Paulson had concluded that the ostensibly roaring US housing market was in trouble. He approached Goldman Sachs to help structure a deal that would allow him to bet against subprime mortgages. Such bets can take a variety of forms. The one Paulson was after was a complex, synthetic construction of the type described above. If done properly, it could magnify his gains. Paulson was looking to short US subprime property CDOs by arranging swaps with issuers of such instruments.

Goldman Sachs happened to know a party who would be interested in such a swap: the German bank IKB Deutsche Industriebank AG (IKB). It would be a continuation of an established business relationship. Back in 2004 IKB commissioned Goldman to design a CDO, backed by a predesignated set of residential mortgage-backed securities (RMBSs). In those first deals – where the Abacus brand was first used – IKB found its own counterparties to take the short side of the deal.

Abacus 2007-AC1 would differ from those earlier structures. A typical insurance deal of that sort is provided against underlying assets selected by outsiders. IKB agreed to provide such insurance only if the underlying assets were selected by outsiders, on the assumption that those outsiders take the bulk of the risk and pay only for insurance. Knowing full well that IKB would sign to a deal only if the underlying assets were selected by an outsider, Goldman invited ACA Management LLC, a unit of a bond insurer, to help select the securities. The key to the scheme, and to the scam as alleged by the SEC, was ACA collaboration with Goldman and Paulson in the selection of the securities. ACA agreed to do so, believing that Paulson was a client who wished to own some of the riskiest parts of the securities. Paulson's motivation was exactly the opposite: he wanted to bet against the assets selected. With that aim, he hoped to pick up the riskiest possible. In the event, to ACA's credit, over half of the 123 securities picked by Paulson were vetoed by ACA.[2]

On 12 February 2007 ACA finalized its agreement to participate as the selection agent, and around a fortnight later the final reference portfolio was agreed by both ACA and Paulson. The deal contained about ninety RMBS bonds of approximately equal size, worth around $2bn. Goldman then put together the deal between IKB and Paulson. IKB was not aware that Paulson's interest was in shorting the deal. IKB took $150m of the risk from subprime mortgage bonds in late April 2007. ABN AMRO took some $909m of exposure as well, buying protection on its exposure from an ACA Management affiliate, ACA Financial Guaranty Corp, in May 2007. Paulson immediately shorted the portfolio for more than $1bn of securities. It took only a few months for IKB to lose almost all of its $150m investment. By late 2007 ABN – acquired by then by a consortium of banks including RBS – had lost its bet costing $840.1m. Paulson made about $1bn in total from the deal.

The SEC's case against Goldman Sachs was based on the notion that the bank had fundamentally broken the trust required between associates involved in a deal. Goldman appeared to have deliberately designed a security that it knew would fail, and had acted in an unethical manner in aiding and abetting Paulson to make money at the expense of IKB and ACA. The deal's brochures did not mention Paulson's role in selecting the portfolio that he was intending to short, and were therefore seen as misleading. Moreover, in the SEC's view, Goldman had 'misled ACA into believing that Paulson was investing in the equity of Abacus 2007-AC1 and therefore shared a long interest with CDO investors'.[3]

To make a watertight case, the SEC would have needed to demonstrate that Goldman Sachs had actively misrepresented the situation. Specifically, the SEC needed proof of violations of Section 10(b) of the Exchange Act (and specifically Rule 10b-5) and of Section 17 of the Securities Act.[4]

Goldman made only $15m from the deal. Considering the potential damage to its reputation, sabotaging IKB and ABN AMRO in this case, the deal does not appear like a smart move by Goldman. The very announcement of the civil suit had resulted in a 13 per cent dent in Goldman Sachs's share price in one day alone, entailing a $10bn hit to its market value.[5] Goldman ended up paying $550m in damages, of which $300m were fines to the Treasury, and the rest to ACA and IKB.[6]

This looks like a case of an own goal. Why, then, did Goldman go to the trouble of sabotaging two of its largest clients, for very little value?

One explanation for Goldman's behaviour comes from the official ending of this story. Goldman reached a 'deferred prosecution agreement' with the authorities, under which it neither admitted nor denied guilt. Observers believed that it was a way to placate the unwanted attention to the bank and avert any other scandals coming to surface. Another explanation is technical. Wall Street experts believe that had the case proceeded to court hearings, Goldman may have won it. The technical language in the legal documentation furnishing the deal, and ambiguities in legal concepts, would have helped the bank defend its case and expose the clients as naïve and authorities as politically biased. Legally, Goldman did nothing wrong with Abacus 2007-AC1. The transaction, as far as Goldman was concerned, was not a big deal. In fact, Matt Levine, a Wall Street insider, insists that it is inaccurate to say that Goldman sold synthetic CDOs to investors and secretly bet against them. The synthetic CDO *was* the bet against them![7]

Another explanation was strategic: Goldman had been developing its CDOs business under the Abacus brand name, which it used widely and applied to sixteen different kinds of synthetic CDOs, worth $10bn of securities in all. That Paulson was prepared to 'hire' the brand name for a fee, albeit of $15m, was of strategic business interest to Goldman. The bank's strategy overall could probably be described as a success – until the SEC intervened. By 2007 Goldman was the fourth-largest underwriter of CDOs.[8] In essence, the Abacus deals were all fairly typical synthetic CDOs. 'Abacus,' in other words, was not a one-off affair; nor was it tailored to target the IKB specifically.

Goldman's website describes the company's mission: 'Our people are our greatest asset – we say it often and with good reason. It is only with the determination and dedication of our people that we can serve our clients, generate long-term value for our shareholders and contribute to the broader public.' The 'People and Culture' section continues: 'At the crux of our efforts is a focus on cultivating and sustaining a diverse work environment and workforce, which is critical to meeting the unique needs of our diverse client base and the communities in which we operate.'[9]

'Our People Are Our Greatest Asset'

A manager of a family's investment portfolio recently told us: 'We never agree to meet Goldman Sachs. Those guys are, simply, the best. They are so smooth. We know we will end up signing up to one of their schemes, and we know we are going to lose. Best not to meet them at all.' There is a price to pay for working with a prestigious organization like Goldman, we were told, and it is rarely Goldman that pays it.

6

'A SIMPLE PREMISE'

Wells Fargo

With crisis always comes an opportunity. The continuing rise of the wealth management sector, which has been developing rapidly since 2009, has opened up new and ample opportunities to sabotage not only the owners of small and medium businesses, but the super-rich too.

Let's take Wells Fargo. America's third-largest bank provides an effective case study. It has managed to feature in three scandals, almost synchronously. First, in the footsteps of Gogol's Chichikov and RBS, Wells Fargo staff had been forging not the signatures of clients, but *clients* themselves: two million fake clients, since 2011. Second – and this sounds rather mundane – the bank's intermediates exploited the structure of transactions to force unwanted insurance products on car owners. Third, the bank's asset management – the division that cares for the super-wealthy – has been harvesting its clients for fees that often were not disclosed or authorized, applying them on unwanted or dreamed-up services.

In 2016 revelations surfaced that since 2011 Wells Fargo secretly had been creating millions of unauthorized bank and credit card accounts – without its customers' knowledge.[1] The bank's employees went so far as to create phony PINs and fake email addresses to enrol fictitious customers in their online banking services. The phony accounts earned the bank unwarranted fees and allowed Wells Fargo employees to boost their sales figures to make more money. Over 1.5 million deposit accounts were created which may not have been authorized.

On the face of it, there is no value in phony accounts. As Chichikov himself would note, they require resources to maintain them and create additional paperwork. Why, then, did Wells Fargo's staff think it was a lucrative business? Bonuses is the trivial answer.

The method was simple. Bank employees moved funds from customers' existing accounts into newly created ones without customers' knowledge or consent. As there was not enough money in the original accounts, customers were then being charged for insufficient funds or overdraft fees. Wells Fargo employees also submitted applications for 565,443 credit card accounts without the customers' knowledge or consent. Roughly 14,000 of those accounts incurred over $400,000 in fees, including annual fees, interest charges and overdraft fees.[2] When the dealings finally came to the surface in September 2016, some 5,300 employees were fired and the CEO was ousted. Wells Fargo committed to a 'new standard of behaviour as required by the regulator'.[3]

At Wells Fargo insurance mis-selling predates the phony accounts. The scheme here, again, is very trivial. Drivers in US must carry a policy when they borrow money to buy a new car. It pays out to the bank when the car is stolen or destroyed. Wells Fargo required drivers to carry their own policies but had a right to 'force-place' a policy on borrowers who let insurance lapse. Insurers working for Wells Fargo pushed policies on to 570,000 customers who already had coverage. The abuse goes back to 2005. Wells Fargo estimates it will need to refund $145m to borrowers and adjust account balances by another $37m.[4]

Wells Fargo's brokerage division was known for sales goals, and for payouts that were higher than those of industry peers such as Morgan Stanley and Bank of America.[5] As would transpire in 2018, wealth advisers frequently targeted wealthy clients in Wells Fargo's private bank, sometimes steering them into alternative investment funds of which Wells Fargo was the majority owner, again without clients' knowledge. Clients' money was shifted between products such as certificates of deposit and structured notes, typically to earn higher bank fees. Clients with assets of more than $2m were funnelled into a higher-fee platform known as Investment and Fiduciary Services. Wells Fargo often mandated client quotas for riskier alternative investments, such as private equity and hedge funds, regardless of whether they were appropriate. Wealthier clients were often placed in the GAI Agility Income Fund or the GAI Corbin Multi-Strategy Fund, which are majority owned by Wells Fargo and from which the bank could also collect management fees. The East Valley region of Phoenix was a hotbed for these problems, according to current and former employees.[6]

In many cases, once customers signed the relevant paperwork, advisers could make multiple changes to accounts without updating them, normally triggering additional fees.[7] Then there was something that was internally known as 'churning': some advisers would redeem clients from annuities that had large surrender charges and would place them into another product with annual fees of 1–1.5 per cent.[8]

Another tactic at Wells Fargo Advisors revolved around the bank's Envision financial-planning software. Some advisers would run the Envision simulations without their clients being present by plugging in numbers they knew would recommend investments that clients already held. One whistleblower told of employees writing in fake or inaccurate client information to boost their plan numbers towards deferred compensation as recently as 2016.[9]

Having admitted to the SEC to defrauding thousands of customers, Wells Fargo explained its vision on its website:

> We want to satisfy our customers' financial needs and help them succeed financially… This unites us around a simple premise: Customers can be better served when they have a relationship with a trusted provider that knows them well, provides reliable guidance, and can serve their full range of financial needs.[10]

Sabotaging clients is common in the banking industry. So common, in fact, that scientific terms are usually invoked to explain why sabotage can occur. Asymmetric information about a product (like in the interest rate swaps of RBS); lack of financial literacy or sophistication (as in the Abacus affair); individuation of risk (in any transaction, where the risk is ultimately with the client); the principal-agent dilemma that explains the conflict of interest between the agent and the client. In reality, the conflict is encoded in the very operation of modern finance. Unavoidably, it means that the customer of the financial institution is at a disadvantage in dealing with the institution.

The cases described above provide only very few illustrations of a general trend. Some observers will inevitably want to attribute the behaviour to isolated rogue elements within specific banks, operating on their own initiative. But we are much more pessimistic.

As Paul Samuelson argued many years back, the efficient market hypothesis suggests that neither banks nor other financial institutions can make money just because of their superior ability to interpret financial trends. The alternative and better-guaranteed source of income, to come back to the legendary quips emerging from Lehman's meeting, is to take advantage of the 'dumbest person in the room'. And the dumbest person in the room is typically the customer: the average individual banking with their local branches, or small and medium-size businesses. Rather than treat RBS, Goldman Sachs or Wells Fargo as outliers, regulators should classify the practice of sabotaging customers in the category of 'highly likely' abuse and act accordingly.

In autumn 2018, as investigations into abusive practices at RBS and HBOS were concluding, UK Finance, a lobby group for the banking industry, commissioned its own report on the scandals. It recommended strengthening the financial ombudsman and lifting the maximum payout to £600,000. The report also said small businesses could rely on banks' voluntary compensation schemes.[11]

PART THREE

HOSTICIDE: SABOTAGING EACH OTHER

Every year, *Fortune* magazine produces a ranking of the world's most admired companies and financial institutions. This index is not known for analytical accuracy or staggering prophesy. It merely aggregates the prevailing opinions of 3,000 or so leading business insiders. In the summer of 2007 the judgement of the 'Street' ranked Lehman Brothers by far the best-run bank in the world, placing it first in practically every aspect of the business. Lehman topped the chart in innovation, people management, the use of corporate assets, social responsibility, quality of management, financial soundness, long-term investment and quality of products/services. Lehman was followed by Bear Stearns and Goldman Sachs.

The unfolding meltdown would soon claim both Lehman Brothers and Bear Stearns as its casualties. It might be a pure coincidence that the institutions which *Fortune* ranked first and second in its 2007 survey were so deeply unlucky as to become the only two large banks to go down in 2007–9. It may have been their sheer bad luck that, unlike AIG and many others, the US government was not prepared to bail them out. It may have been an accident, too, that the third on the list, Goldman Sachs, has topped the chart ever since.

Or, maybe, not an accident.

We are not the only ones to make an allusion, so far unproven, to the role Goldman and its alumni serving in the US government at the time have played in the downfall of Lehman and Bear Stearns.[1] Yet while specifics remain unproven, the general principle is well understood by insiders.

Theoretically, financial economics is concerned primarily with issues of competition and efficiency, access to financing and stability in the financial system. But, in reality, there is also another type of competition taking place, which has little to do with the above. We refer to the ruthless, if not brutal, game of competitive sabotage among financial institutions, orchestrated by CEOs and top managers in the banking system, and supported, abated or foiled by hosts of powerful players such as hedge funds. This competitive game has little to do with economics, or with the efficient delivery of services in the financial system. In fact, the field of financial economics offers little that can shed light on such games. It is a game of hosticide and survival, where the victorious feast on the remains of their prey, generating a considerable portion of their profits that way.

The sabotage strategies employed by banks and other financial institutions are aimed at destroying competitors and building 'fat' as they prepare for the next encounter. The ultimate prize in the game is becoming too big to fail, a major tactic of sabotaging the state which we discuss in part four. At the same time, banks and financial institutions need each other as counterparties. Otherwise, they would not have a business at all. The game of sabotage is, therefore, intricate and complex. Its objective is not a complete monopoly but, rather, a *relative monopoly*, a position where competitors are weakened and moved way down in the pecking order.

We start with the story of Bear Stearns. The second-most-admired bank in the *Fortune* 2007 survey that collapsed in 2008, only to be bought by one of its main competitors. While ostensibly a story of financial inefficiency and profligacy, the implosion of Bear may be read as a case of collaborative sabotage by its peers.

7

WHO LET THE BEAR DOWN?

The consensus, on the eve of the crisis, was that Bear Stearns was not that different from other players in its exposure to bad debt. Yet, along with Lehman a year later, it was allowed to go under. A detailed examination of Bear's failure suggests it was not only about financial insolvency. Instead we find multiple, strangely connected incidents that make the case for collaborative sabotage orchestrated, most probably, by Goldman Sachs.

Bear Stearns was established in 1927 but became a publicly listed company only in 1985.[1] By the 1990s it acted as a broker and clearing house for other financial institutions. 'Lean, scrappy and hungry for profits', Bear was not particularly liked by its peers. *Street Fighters*, a bestselling story of the bank's collapse, describes Bear as a bank that 'cared little for appearances'.[2] Bear seemed to have enjoyed its reputation as the bad boy of Wall Street, proudly hiring castoffs from other firms, providing 'geisha girls' to escort visitors to meetings and refusing to follow the crowd in its business conduct.[3]

In one version of events, the collaborative sabotage that ultimately pulled down Bear Stearns began long before the summer of 2007. This story begins on 17 August 1998, the day the Russian government defaulted on all its outstanding debt, exposing foreign investors to losses in the multimillions. The Russian default amplified panic in the world financial markets. One of its most significant casualties would be the Long Term Capital Management (LTCM) fund, a boutique hedge fund run by two Nobel Prize winners in economics.[4] The Nobel Prizes were awarded for the partners' work on the Black–Scholes formula, used until today for calculating the prices of financial derivatives. But Russia's default unleashed volatility on a scale far beyond what the model was designed for. Having previously been hit by the Asian crisis, LTCM suffered losses of $553m in one day. This was equivalent to 15 per cent of its capital. Within one month, it lost almost $2bn. Unable to alter its positions, LTCM was going down.

The implosion of the institution would be a major blow, not merely to LTCM and its founders, but to Wall Street as a whole. Too much of what Wall Street was about – smart finance, the power of financial engineering, connections, reputation – was at stake with the fund's collapse. The Fed decided it had to step in and shore LTCM up. Alan Greenspan, the Fed's then chair, asked fourteen major banks that served as prime brokers[5] to contribute to a private bailout of LTCM.[6] Thirteen did agree, but Bear's CEO, Jimmy Cayne, refused to chip in.

In fact, compounding the stress, Bear called in $500m. The other Wall Street firms had no choice but to pay an additional $50m each on top of the agreed $250m contribution to the bailout package.[7] In a last attempt to make Bear contribute, it was threatened with the loss of LTCM's clearing business. Jimmy Cayne reportedly replied: 'You told me we wouldn't clear, I agree.

We're not. By the way, if you want to hire us back, it's triple the rate.'[8]

Memory is a funny thing in finance. We often hear that Wall Street and the City are short on institutional memory. Mistakes are quickly forgotten, and the new generation of financiers rarely has any knowledge, much less recollection, of the experience of their predecessors. But in this particular case the Fed and the other major banks would not forget the incident. Ten years later, so the fable goes, they refused to bail Cayne's company out of trouble, just as Bear refused to do the same to those in trouble back in 1998.

There is, no doubt, an element of truth in this version of the story. But the evidence suggests that some banks and hedge funds, led by Goldman Sachs, not only refused to help with the bailout of Bear Stearns but may have triggered Bear's troubles in the first place.

Like many in the industry, Bear Stearns was unprepared for the impending crisis. In its 2006 annual report the bank bragged about its results: 'We ranked number one for the third consecutive year in US mortgage-backed securities underwriting, secured the top spot in the securitization of adjustable-rate mortgages, and ranked in the top five of global collateralized debt obligations (CDO) market.'[9]

In reality, however, Bear's balance sheet was deteriorating. Two of its in-house hedge funds, High Grade Fund and Enhanced Leverage Fund, ran by Ralph Cioffi and Matt Tannin, loaded up on MBSs at precisely the wrong moment. From 2003 Cioffi and Tannin had been losing money in each of their funds. By February 2007 they began to worry about their exposure to the subprime mortgage market. Earlier that month New Century Financial, a major mortgage lender, reduced its earnings forecasts due to an improper valuation of its mortgages transactions.[10] By March 2007 twenty-five mortgage lenders across the US 'had gone out of business, declared bankruptcy, put themselves up for sale, or announced significant losses'.[11]

Untruthfully, Bear insisted that its exposure to MBS was insignificant.[12] Despite reassurances, the performance of the two hedge funds quickly worsened. On 17 July 2007 Bear Stearns finally announced the closure of the two funds; on 3 August 2007 Standard & Poor's publicly signalled that the two failed funds could cause problems for the parent company, downgrading the Bear Stearns credit from stable to negative.[13]

What happened over the next few months is usually described as a roller coaster. Aware of Cayne's reputation on Wall Street,[14] Bear replaced him with a new CEO, Alan Schwartz, in January 2008. Schwartz was looking forward to announcing that Bear had made a profit of $1 per share in the first quarter of the year.[15] With roughly $18bn in cash, Bear's liquidity ratio was beyond what was required by regulators. In other words, by early 2008 Bear seemed to have recovered from the collapse of its two hedge funds.

But in early March 2008 rumours began to spread that Bear and Lehman were heavily exposed to toxic debt. Some of the rumours are traceable to an analysis by one hedge fund, Atlantic Advisors, whose president calculated that the cost of insuring the obligations of Bear Stearns and Lehman Brothers, or CDSs, had increased rapidly in a single month. The hedge fund president concluded: 'In my book they are insolvent.'[16] Another key adviser employed by many leading hedge funds, Bob Sloan of S3 Partners, reached a similar verdict. By March 2008 Sloan's clients had withdrawn $25bn from Bear.[17]

Who Let the Bear Down?

Bear's fatal week began late on a frozen day, Friday, 7 March 2008, when a major European bank[18] declined Bear's request for a short-term $2bn loan.[19] 'Being denied such a loan is the Wall Street equivalent of having your buddy refuse to front you $5 the day before pay day,' *Fortune* wrote.[20] On the following Monday a major rating agency downgraded all MBSs issued by Bear.[21] On Tuesday, 11 March, the Fed announced that it would make $200bn in Treasury securities available for struggling securities firms, starting on 27 March.[22] Investors drew the conclusion that the Federal Reserve was preparing to bail out a failing securities firm, and Bear Stearns appeared to be a likely institution of concern.

That very Tuesday, Bear's new CFO, Samuel L. Molinaro, went on CNBC to dispel the rumours about Bear's position: 'There is no liquidity crisis. No margin calls. It's nonsense,' he said emphatically. As he was on air, three major Wall Street banks, Goldman Sachs, Credit Suisse and Deutsche Bank, received a large amount of novation requests for Bear Stearns from hedge funds, among them Citadel Investment and Paulson & Co.[23] Novation requests enable financial firms to sell a contract which transfers credit risk to a third party in exchange for a fee. The timing of those novation requests, and the fact that they were triggered by hedge funds and sent only to three banks, is a cause célèbre for the conspiracy theorists. Subsequently, Bear Stearns's CEO, Alan Schwartz, would feign surprise that all novation requests were sent to the same three firms, implying that those requests were part of a concerted attack mounted by those hedge funds on Bear.[24]

Goldman and Credit Suisse executives tried to curtail the torrent by telling their traders to hold all Bear Stearns novation requests. But that only made things worse. Credit Suisse issued a memo to stop the novation requests for Bear in 'a "blast" email to many of its trading staff which became the subject of widespread rumours and gossip'.[25] Goldman went even further, informing at least two of its hedge fund clients that it would no longer stand in for trades with Bear.[26] The two Wall Street banks were announcing to the world they had lost trust in their major trading partner.

Kyle Bass from the hedge fund Hayman Capital was among those clients to receive the Goldman email. Subsequently he confessed to being 'astounded' to receive the news. He rang a friend at Goldman to confirm the authenticity of the message. The message he received back was that Goldman 'were done with Bear, that there was too much risk. That was the end for them.'[27]

On Wednesday, 12 March, the Goldman and Credit Suisse emails were leaked to the outside world. A CNBC interview with Bear Stearns's CEO, Alan Schwartz, compounded the situation, as the events of the day before were made public. The CNBC journalist told Schwartz that he had direct knowledge of a trader whose credit department had held up a trade with Bear Stearns due to concerns about the bank's health.[28] Although the trade eventually went through, the damage was done: it now was public knowledge that major Wall Street institutions did not trust Bear. The interview triggered a full run on the bank. Most hedge funds pulled out their investments, affecting the bank's liquidity position. Bear's liquidity declined from $18.1bn on Monday, to $12.4bn on Tuesday, and $3bn by Wednesday lunchtime.[29]

By the afternoon of the next day, the cost of insuring $10m of Bear debt via credit default swaps spiralled beyond $1m, from around $350,000 in the month before. That Tuesday evening banks refused to issue any credit protection for Bear Stearns.[30] If on Thursday morning repo lenders were still happy to trade with Bear, by mid-afternoon they had dropped out as well.[31] By 7 p.m.,

Bear's executives realized that roughly $30bn of repo loans would not be rolled over the next day, leaving the institution $15bn short of what it needed to survive Friday.[32] Bear Steans could only seek an emergency loan or file for bankruptcy the next day.[33]

THE RESCUE

The rescue was arranged on Thursday night. J. P. Morgan Chase, long keen on being a giant, expressed an interest in taking over Bear's primary broker functions. Jamie Dimon, J. P. Morgan's CEO, was called in by Timothy Geithner, then at the New York Fed. J. P. Morgan was not prepared to provide the needed $15bn emergency loan. If the run were to continue the next day, J. P. Morgan could have lost the entire amount. The J. P. Morgan team asked for the Federal Reserve's backing to take on this risk. At 11 p.m. the team of J. P. Morgan executives arrived at Bear Stearns's headquarters to assess the situation. By 4 a.m. an arrangement was found: J. P. Morgan would loan Bear Stearns the funds, which J. P. Morgan borrowed from the central bank. The loan was extended for twenty-eight days.[34]

The next day, Friday, seemed to have started well: the markets did not appear to be fazed over the overnight deal. It would be a few hours later that the storm hit. The bank run escalated, and Bear's capital reserves depleted quickly. On the evening of Friday the 14th, Hank Paulson, Treasury Secretary, called Bear's CEO. Paulson threatened to cut the credit line granted the night before if Schwartz did not arrange a takeover by Sunday. Over the weekend several bidders engaged in talks with Bear's executives, but all eventually dropped out. Even J. P. Morgan did not want to buy the bank. Having done some research, J. P. Morgan realized that

Bear was worth only $236m. That was just one-fifth the value of its headquarters building.[35] Hank Paulson and Timothy Geithner had to convince Jamie Dimon at J. P. Morgan that he could get a cheap deal, guaranteed by the central bank. Bear was eventually sold for $2 a share, an offer that was later upgraded to $10. A year earlier Bear Stearns shares had been trading at $170.[36]

Was Bear's downfall inevitable? Many in the industry see Bear's spectacular demise as highly unusual. Rumours often do circulate on Wall Street and can normally be fended off with the help of other players in the industry vouching for the institution in trouble. Despite low liquidity, the day-by-day business of Bear Stearns could have gone on as usual for a limited period of time. Indeed, never before had a bank become a victim of rumours alone. Usually a collapse of such dimensions is triggered by a major scandal or an indictment. Worse, the collapse at this point was unnecessary. If hedge funds had stuck to their trades with Bear for thirteen more days, the Fed facility announced on Tuesday, 11 March 2008, would have made sure Bear secured high-quality US Treasuries in exchange for any illiquid holdings of mortgage-backed securities.[37]

Bear Stearns's own staff believe the demise of the bank was an act of sabotage. Its former CEO Jimmy Cayne stated publicly that rumours of liquidity problems were deliberately placed: 'Rumour, innuendo. I'm not going to use the word "conspiracy", but it's part of it,' said Cayne in his testimony.[38] Alan Schwartz, CEO in charge during the collapse, did not mince his words either, singling out Goldman Sachs for the concerted attack that led to Bear's demise. Schwartz confronted Goldman's CEO, Lloyd Blankfein, about it.[39] Bear Stearns's executives believed that Goldman collaborated with several hedge funds to short-sell Bear Stearns stocks, in order to subsequently make a huge profit from its collapse.[40] They handed over documents to the Securities and Exchange Commission for an investigation into insider trading and market manipulation, but the investigation did not find anything substantial.

The data speaks for itself. In the three weeks preceding Bear's collapse, Goldman and the hedge funds Citadel Investment and Paulson & Co. exited about 400 trades with Bear Stearns – more than with any other firm.[41] Inside Bear, rumours had been circulating all week that Deutsche Bank was shorting (that means betting against) Bear, and that Goldman and Citadel were determined to bring Bear down.[42] A vice-chairman of an unnamed major investment bank is quoted as saying:

> I don't know of any firm, no matter the capital, that could have withstood that kind of bombardment by the shorts. This was not about capital. It was about people losing confidence, spurred on by rumours fueled by people who had an interest in the fall of Bear Stearns... if I had to pick the biggest financial crime ever perpetuated, I would say, "Bear Stearns."[43]

8

—

WHAT GOES AROUND COMES AROUND

The Rise and Fall of RBS

On the other side of the Atlantic, banking hosticide was escalating just as the financial system was breaking down in 2008. In what follows, we recount the Royal Bank of Scotland's strange and, ultimately, fatal decision to mount the largest banking takeover ever: namely, the hostile takeover of the ailing Dutch bank, ABN AMRO, right in the middle of the largest crisis since 1929. The £48bn ($70bn) deal struck was the largest-ever merger in financial services. It would become the 'nail in the coffin' of RBS, which had to be taken over by the British government in 2009. The merger is often described as a case of rushed judgement and incomplete homework by RBS. But there was more than poor judgement behind RBS's fateful acquisition of ABN AMRO. It appears that RBS was pushed over by active acts of sabotage perpetrated by its erstwhile partner, Santander, and probably Barclays too.

In 1992 George Mathewson became the chief executive of RBS. Mathewson was a man with a plan. His great idea was to turn RBS from a potential appetizer on the menu of some predator bank to a large roaming predator, safe in the knowledge that it had turned itself into a too-big-to-fail mammoth. Mathewson's timing was perfect: the 1986 Building Societies Act removed industry restrictions, allowing building societies to demutualize and compete with other High Street Banks. The old 'gentlemanly' agreement between Scottish banks and banks in the rest of Britain – which restrained banks to their home regions – also ceased to be upheld.[1]

In 1987 the Midland Bank, one of the big four UK banks, was partly acquired by the Hongkong and Shanghai Banking Corporation, better known as HSBC. It was a wake-up call for the new RBS. At that moment RBS did not have the capacity to acquire the Midland, but Mathewson was set to change all this.[2] It was not long before RBS plucked up the courage and itself tried to acquire several building societies, most of which were eventually bought by the other big banks. The largest banks sliced up the British banking industry without remorse. Those who failed to wolf down others would soon fall prey themselves. Both Scottish banks, the Royal Bank of Scotland (RBS) and the Bank of Scotland, had been pursued by English banks. In 2001 the Bank of Scotland merged with the Halifax to become Halifax Bank of Scotland (HBOS), which, in turn, was taken over by Lloyds in 2008 – another sombre story of intrigue and sabotage. HSBC made attempts to acquire RBS in 1982 and then once again in 1996. By the late 1990s RBS was on the menu of several banks.[3]

The only option left to RBS was to join the higher ranks of the banking elite and thus save itself from hostile takeovers. Initially RBS contemplated a hostile takeover of Barclays. Eventually it settled for NatWest – one of the remaining 'big three' in Britain. Although it was known as the 'beached whale' that lurched from one crisis to another, NatWest was still *three times* RBS's size.[4] To engage in the bidding war for NatWest, RBS had to 'stretch every pound', raising its debt-to-equity ratio to dangerously high levels.[5] According to observers at the time, the £21bn takeover had little economic logic behind it, and was mainly a 'defensive manoeuvre' against other predators coming for RBS itself. RBS's strategy for the costly merger was simple: 'fire most people at NatWest and extract the most value from its 6 million customers.'[6] We discussed some of the fruits of the takeover in Chapter 4.

The takeover of NatWest by RBS became the stuff of legends and a classic Harvard Business School case on mergers and acquisitions. As far as RBS was concerned, the acquisition was a risk worth taking. It elevated RBS into the ranks of global players. It became the third-biggest bank in the UK and seventh in Europe.[7] In 2007 it would peak as the world's largest bank.

The merger with NatWest elevated another figure in RBS into the highest ranks, Fred Goodwin. Goodwin played one of the key roles in the NatWest takeover, but soon wanted a 'NatWest success' deal signed under his own name. His choice was to take on Barclays in a bidding war. The target was the ailing ABN AMRO, one of the largest banks based in the Netherlands.

The takeover of ABN AMRO had no economic substance. Fred Goodwin would later admit that it was 'screamingly obvious that the deal was mediocre at best'.[8] For RBS, it would prove to be an act of suicide by hosticide.

What Goes Around Comes Around

Early in 2007 rumours began to swirl that either RBS or Barclays would soon be snapped up by 'an' American bank. J. P. Morgan Chase and Citigroup were mentioned. When Goodwin learned that Barclays was in talks with ABN AMRO, he concluded that such a deal would leave RBS vulnerable, likely to be taken over by one of the American banks.[9] By then RBS had been pursuing ABN's subsidiary LaSalle, an investment bank boutique in the US, for a while. LaSalle was the jewel in ABN's crown. It would have elevated RBS into the top league of global and American investment banking. It appears, however, that yet again RBS's attempted takeover of ABN AMRO was motivated less by economic logic, and instead aimed at preventing its rival, Barclays, from getting its way.

Strategic considerations, and in particular the goal of thwarting Barclays' ABN AMRO talks, led to overvaluation of ABN AMRO. ABN's CEO, Rijkman Groenink, favoured a friendly merger with Barclays. In order to match Barclays' offer, RBS formed a consortium, relying on its long-term business partner, the Spanish Banco Santander, and a smaller Belgian-Dutch bank, Fortis. This would prove to be another fatal mistake. The Barclays merger with ABN talks had been secret but friendly, and Barclays therefore had access to ABN AMRO's books.[10] RBS, in contrast, launched a hostile takeover bid and thus had sparse access to ABN's books. Goodwin went on a wind-and-a-prayer approach offering cash and seeking, in turn, a 'due-diligence light' approach.[11] In July 2007 Barclays' CEO, John Varley, made the final offer of €67.6bn for ABN AMRO, largely based on shares. The news emerged just after the RBS consortium published its offer of €71.1bn, based largely on cash. Unsurprisingly, shareholders of ABN, most notably its hedge fund investors, favoured a high cash payout over the Barclays offer.

For RBS, the deal turned pretty rotten pretty quickly. In October 2007 LaSalle – the primary reason for RBS's interest in ABN AMRO – was sold to the Bank of America. Having lost the crown jewels, the RBS consortium faced higher costs than initially expected. Worse, although the merged bank could have been split up between consortium partners,[12] the Dutch central bank required RBS to take full responsibility for ABN as a whole. In other words, the risk was truly with RBS and not with the consortium.[13]

Goodwin tried to pull out of the takeover twice. First, in mid-July 2007, when the Dutch Supreme Court confirmed that ABN was allowed to sell LaSalle,[14] and then again in August. But RBS was entrapped by the legal agreement it signed with its consortium partners. Lawyers advised RBS that withdrawal would 'unleash a torrent of litigation, from both RBS's consortium partners and ABN's shareholders'.[15] The partners on the consortium had too much to win from this deal. While Fortis actually did consider pulling out, Merrill Lynch acted as sole adviser on the transaction, earning $600m in fees from the success of the takeover.[16] Santander, RBS's supposedly long-term partner, threatened with lawsuits if the agreement was not upheld. Santander also had plans to resell its part in ABN, and Merrill Lynch was counting on several hundred million in fees.

WITH FRIENDS LIKE THESE . . .

The ABN deal marked the triumphant result of a long-term collaboration between Banco Santander and RBS. Both Santander and RBS started out as provincial banks. But once the sector turned competitive, the two banks struck a deal. In October 1988 RBS and Santander formed a strategic alliance, involving cross shareholdings[17] between the banks and directors of each bank sitting on the board of the other. The long-term collaboration centred on joint ventures and other business opportunities.[18]

Emilio Botín, who took over as CEO of the Spanish lender from his father in 1986, catapulted the bank from Spain's number six bank in assets to number one in both Spain and Latin America.[19] Similarly to Mathewson at RBS, Botín redefined his bank's strategy towards expansion. In 1992 he captured the controlling stake in Banesto (Banco Español de Crédito), a first major acquisition followed by many more deals in Spain and worldwide. By 2015 Santander was making 87 per cent of its profit outside Spain.[20] Its targets were Latin America and the UK. Today the UK is the largest contributor to Santander's earnings.

RBS and Santander decided to collaborate to survive in the hosticidal culture of banking. The alliance provided RBS with an informal high-level forum at which Mathewson and a colleague could compare notes and mull over strategic options with their Santander counterparts.[21] Their combined strategy aimed to grab larger and larger slices of the British banking sector when and where opportunities arose. Santander ended up taking over three demutualized building societies: Abbey (2004), Alliance & Leicester (2008) and parts of Bradford & Bingley (2008). By the end of their collaboration, however, Santander was the only one left smiling. The ABN deal had secured Santander ABN AMRO's Brazilian unit, Banco Real, which made Santander the fourth-most-important lender there. They also wanted to resell the Italian unit, Banca Antonveneta, to Monte dei Paschi di Siena for €9bn, after it had been valued at just €6.6bn.[22] Alfred Saenz, Santander's chief executive, said bluntly: 'We have got the best bits of ABN AMRO; we got the best meat from the kill. We are the only ones coming out smiling.'[23]

After the takeover was complete, Botín, Santander's victorious CEO, refused to take phone calls from Goodwin.[24] A three-decade-long partnership had ended. Unlike RBS, Santander survived the global financial crisis relatively well – mainly due to its focus on retail banking and little exposure to US subprime mortgage debt.[25] Indeed, from January 2009 the Spanish bank had lobbied the European Commission to launch an investigation into 'state aid' given to the nationalized Lloyds Bank and its old ally, RBS. Santander's aim in lobbying the European Commission was to achieve 'a break up of both RBS and Lloyds so he could cherry-pick the best bits at fire-sale prices'.[26]

The strategy worked: in 2009 Santander was allowed by the authorities in London and Brussels to bid for RBS business branches called Williams & Glyn.[27] In pursuit of cheap deals, Santander pulled out of the bidding competition several times but stated that it 'may return to the negotiating table if the Edinburgh-based lender is prepared to lower its asking price'.[28] If the ABN takeover was the 'nail in the coffin' for RBS, then Santander was key in manoeuvring RBS into this deadly corner.

BARCLAYS GETS THE UPPER HAND

It is less clear what motivated Barclays to pursue the bidding for ABN AMRO for so long. Barclays knew that RBS was about to buy an overvalued ABN, but as long as Barclays stayed in the race, the costs for its rival would remain high. This, in turn, came to the benefit of ABN's hedge fund shareholders and surely also to Barclays. Retrospective evaluation of the RBS books shows that without the acquisition of ABN the Scottish bank would have more or less broken even between 2008 and the first half of 2009.

ABN accounted for 75–144 per cent (depending on different estimates) of the combined group's operating losses in the same period.[29]

So did Barclays put RBS on the path to collapse? It may be that Barclays played a very clever game. Or perhaps it was sheer good luck. Barclays certainly appears to have tried to compete with RBS. Barclays Capital, for instance, sought to rally several hedge funds to weaken the consortium partner Fortis by short-selling its shares 'and kill its planned €13.5bn rights issue'.[30] This could have destroyed the position of the consortium, but the strategy failed because most hedge funds were betting in favour of ABN shares and preferred that the RBS consortium keep their price high.

In any case, by August 2007 Barclays' own share price fell, reducing the value of its share-based offer even more. The British lender required the Bank of England stand-by facility to borrow an unusually high amount of £1.6bn at a penal rate of 6.75 per cent.[31] Although Barclays blamed the liquidity injection on a technical breakdown in the clearing system, it was the second time in two weeks that Barclays had to rely on the mechanism. Days prior to the drop in share price, several leading figures left Barclays Capital. They were in charge of collateralized debt obligations (CDOs) and the construction of structured investment vehicles (SIVs).[32] A departure of high-ranking staff sent jitters through the global financial markets and was an early indicator of Barclays's exposure towards toxic American debt. This was confirmed a few months later when Barclays had to raise capital to avoid a government bailout. Starting in June 2008, it received a total of £6.1bn in two payments, from Qatari and Singaporean investors.[33]

As the Barclays share price dropped, it could no longer compete with the RBS-led consortium. Yet although Barclays knew what was on the books of ABN – more toxic debt – it kept its position in the race for ABN up to October 2007. Observers at the time were puzzled. The *Telegraph* wrote: 'It seems extraordinary that Barclays and RBS are so desperate to buy this second division bank at such a massive premium when the world's best banks, such as Goldman Sachs and Morgan Stanley, are off 14pc and 27pc respectively in the past month.'[34] Most experts agreed that ABN's share price had been overvalued because of the bidding competition. It was estimated: 'Without the bid interest ABN shares would probably plummet 40pc.'[35]

On 5 October 2007 Barclays officially pulled out. By that time the financial crisis had already engulfed Bear Stearns and Northern Rock. Observers saw the obvious disadvantages of acquiring ABN, but nevertheless recognized that Barclays was under pressure to expand. *The New York Times*, for example, wrote that losing this bid meant that 'Barclays will now have to come up with a plan to continue to grow and meet expectations of investors.'[36] The comment shows, once more, that even in the midst of a crisis the quality of acquired assets mattered little compared to the short-term gains of eliminating competitors.

—

BEWARE GOOD ADVICE

Deutsche's Helping Hand in Iceland

'Think twice before pursuing the €72bn acquisition of ABN AMRO,' John Cryan, then a UBS deals banker, is said to have told RBS in August 2007.[1]

RBS did not heed the advice. In 2015 John Cryan, considered by his peers a very honourable man with strong business ethics,[2] assumed the helm of Deutsche Bank. His task there was not an easy one. The bank's post-2008 earnings have been thin, partly due to large fines and out-of-court settlements with various authorities. The more serious charges against Deutsche included LIBOR rigging, the mis-selling of subprime mortgages before 2007, facilitating mirror deals and, possibly, money laundering out of Russia, and many others. Was the bank bothered by this? An insider recalls Deutsche's internal approach to these risks: 'When issues were found, the approach was "How much are we going to get fined?" If the sum wasn't astronomical, the bank's management appeared willing to run the risk.[3]

Cryan had to address the deep-seated problems of business culture in the bank, as well as the unresolved legacy of the 2008 crisis, in particular, Deutsche's high leverage. He had stripped back high-risk business and slashed bonuses. Under Cryan, in 2016, Deutsche took the unprecedented decision to axe virtually all bonuses due to poor results.[4] John Cryan was not popular among Deutsche's staff. In April 2018 Cryan was ejected from his post by Deutsche's investors.

To appreciate Deutsche's buccaneering spirit, we need go no further than the findings of the Icelandic special prosecutor and the role Deutsche Bank played in the collapse of the Icelandic bank Kaupthing.

The year was 2008, and the Icelandic Kaupthing was in trouble. The third-largest lender in the Nordic region, the bank, with total assets of €58bn in late 2007, had outgrown Iceland itself.[5] Having expanded massively over just four years, Kaupthing widened its lending to foreign counterparties in early 2007, just as the international credit markets started to seize up. One of the reasons why Deutsche came out of the 2007–8 crisis relatively well was the fatal decision of Kaupthing to use Deutsche as an adviser. As is often the case in banking and finance, weaknesses are exploited to buffet someone's bottom line. In Kaupthing, Deutsche found a nice little side earner. The cost was the survival of Kaupthing itself.

One indicator of Kaupthing's coming problems was the widening spreads on its credit default swaps (CDSs). CDSs are financial instruments that serve effectively as insurance contracts on a company's creditworthiness. The buyer of the CDS (who often owns the underlying credit) is insured against a default or a 'negative credit event' affecting the bond on which the CDS is written. When spreads on CDS widen, it means that protection against a possible default becomes more expensive. This, in turn, indicates that a default is, in fact, more likely, and the reference entity is less creditworthy. On the eve of the banking meltdown in the summer of 2007, spreads on Kaupthing CDSs were around 30 basis points. In March 2008 the instruments were trading at around 706 bp.[6] Kaupthing was in trouble.

Kaupthing's directors were more interested in finding ways of resolving the symptoms for the bank's failures – the widening spread on its CDSs – than in dealing with the underlying problem: namely, that the bank was insolvent. Their knight in white armour came in the shape of Deutsche Bank, there for help and advice. As is often the case in the hosticidal world of banking, weaknesses are ruthlessly exploited to make a quick buck. Taking advantage of Kaupthing's difficulties, Deutsche asset stripped whatever and whomever Kaupthing touched, including Kaupthing's clients, the Icelandic government and Kaupthing itself. The story was told a year later by Sigurður Einarsson, chairman of Kaupthing at the time, and confirmed by a 2010 report by the Icelandic Special Investigations Committee (SIC).[7]

Deutsche advised Kaupthing to spend all available liquid funds, most of which were Kaupthing's pension funds, on buying back its own short-term bonds in an attempt to normalize the CDS curve. This amounted to market rigging. Moreover, when liquid funds became scarce, Deutsche began to issue credit so that Kaupthing would be able to continue the scheme. The Icelandic prosecutor's report tells the story.

In the summer of 2008 the idea of a credit-linked note transaction appeared in an email communication from an employee of Deutsche Bank. It states that this would mean a direct impact on the CDS spreads rather than an indirect one, as in the case of buy-backs of an issuer's own notes. It also states that this transaction will be financed. The message concludes by stating that the issue has to be timed right to get the 'most "bang" for the buck'. In email messages exchanged by Sigurdur Einarsson and Hreidar Mar Sigurdsson following this, the two agree that they do not need to involve pension funds, but that there is 'no question' that they should do this.[8]

Deutsche always denied that it advised the market-rigging scheme. It claimed that its role was limited to issuing credit-linked notes to facilitate the transaction. Deutsche professed to have had no knowledge that Kaupthing was financing these notes through its clients. However, the Icelandic side argued that, given the circumstances, Deutsche must have known about it. Not only did Deutsche Bank orchestrate this scheme, but it was also on the other side of the bet. In other words, Deutsche took the position of betting against Kaupthing's performance, while issuing and selling the counterposition. The more money Kaupthing ploughed in, desperate to shore up its CDS spread, the more Deutsche made from betting against Kaupthing. In fact, Deutsche made money from two sides of the transaction: first, from lending to Kaupthing, and, second, by betting against the scheme for which the money was used.

Deutsche also advised on the construction of two British Virgin Islands–registered special investment vehicles (SIVs) named Partridge and Chesterfield. Deutsche's brilliant idea was that the two offshore companies would issue CDSs against those who raised the price of Kaupthing's CDSs – thus deterring those from issuing those widening spreads on CDSs.

The two offshore entities were equally remarkable. According to the Icelandic prosecutors, the scheme worked as follows: Kaupthing provided a €130m loan to the companies that owned Chesterfield in late August 2008, of which €5m were paid to Deutsche in commission. The remaining €125m were used to repay an earlier loan from Kaupthing Luxembourg to Deutsche. A month later a second loan for another €125m was issued. Around the same time, the other SIV, Partridge, received its first round of loans, starting with €130m, of which €125m were used for the transaction, and the remaining €5m were split between Deutsche Bank and Partridge. Partridge received, in addition, another loan of €125m. In total, Kaupthing paid €510m to Deutsche through these transactions.

Amazingly the strategy seemed to have worked for a while. But, given that the offshore companies received loans for their insurances from Kaupthing, the scheme was (a) nothing but a blatant attempt at market manipulation, and (b) would not and could not solve the underlying problem of Kaupthing's deteriorating balance sheet. In fact, it only hastened its demise. Davíðsdóttir writes that 'this loss was entirely predictable if the market turned and Kaupthing went out of business... [and] that it was, according to the OSP, clear from the beginning that the companies should never have received the loans'.[9]

Deutsche came out of the banking crisis in Iceland as the largest creditor to the failing banking system.[10] Remarkably, Deutsche received money even as Kaupthing went belly up. An emergency loan by the Icelandic Central Bank was issued for four days on 6 October 2008 to strengthen Kaupthing's subsidiary KSF (Kaupthing Singer & Friedlander, registered on the Isle of Man) and preventing the mother bank from collapse. Iceland's central bank, however, failed to ensure that the funds were used exclusively for such a purpose. The next day, on 7 October 2008, for reasons not clarified, Kaupthing paid €50m to Deutsche Bank, effectively financed by the Icelandic regulator. The same day Kaupthing was nationalized and the next day, 8 October, the Kaupthing board resigned. Kaupthing's emergency loan was never repaid.[11]

Who gained from this? The sums that Deutsche Bank made overall from the series of acts of sabotage would never be fully determined. Betting on Kaupthing's collapse must have yielded Deutsche Bank a fortune. We will probably never know how much this scheme generated in total, but it is most likely to vastly exceed Deutsche's final settlement fees of €450m.

Kaupthing itself, although claiming the scheme was proposed by Deutsche, is not innocent. The Icelandic prosecutors found a pattern when they looked into earlier instances of Kaupthing's market manipulations and into the case of credit-linked notes issued via Deutsche Bank. Three top managers of Kaupthing were convicted and served time in jail. In the end, however, Kaupthing did pay a high price for its market manipulation, whereas Deutsche Bank came out a true winner. Deutsche Bank has emerged as the largest single claimant against the assets of the failed Kaupthing and is said to be owed almost 900 billion Icelandic krona (£4.8bn) through close to fifty different claims. The bulk of that sum is understood to relate to claims in Deutsche Bank's capacity as custodian bank on behalf of third parties.[12]

A lawsuit in London against Deutsche Bank was meant to recover those ill-gotten gains. But proceedings were awaiting the verdict in Iceland, where the former Kaupthing managers (but not Deutsche Bank) were indicted. The Kaupthing managers ended up in jail, and Deutsche Bank made sure to settle its charges in London. In its 2016 annual report, Deutsche states that it 'has now reached a settlement of the Kaupthing and SPV Proceedings which has been paid in the first quarter of 2017'.[13] The settlement was interpreted as an admission of misconduct. Deutsche had to pay a fine of €450m (compared to €509m claimed by the SIVs in London).[14] The author of the 'bang for the buck' email, who appears to have been the main contact for Kaupthing in his deal, had to leave Deutsche Bank amid the legal proceedings.[15]

PART FOUR

THE BIG, THE BAD AND THE CRYPTO

Sabotaging the State

In economics, the government is an 'exogenous factor'. It is outside the model. This does not mean that governments are unimportant. No serious economist would ever think that. Governments impose all sorts of rules, regulations and taxation, which do affect the bottom line. Profits in the financial system are made in and through financial trading, and the rules, regulations and taxation make it a bit more difficult to make money in finance. One would expect bankers and financiers to take a dim view of them.

To our surprise, however, the majority of the bankers and financiers we spoke to were remarkably sanguine about the constraints imposed by financial regulations. 'Governments provide the rules, and we will work with these rules,' seems to be the prevalent view. The message we kept hearing from financiers was that whichever regulations governments come up with, they should be clear and preferably predictable, and they should not be subject to populist changes of mind.

This seems to be at odds with the popular belief that markets do not want regulation. The impression one often gets from the media and academia is that financiers actively oppose the introduction of rules, regulations and taxation. But in real life bankers and financiers seem less bothered by regulations and taxes than they apparently should be. One possible answer was intimated to us by a chief economist of one of Europe's largest banks in the autumn of 2008: 'I am not worried one bit about new regulations. I have a very good team. It will take them about two hours to come up with a clever solution to any new rules governments might come up with.'

The more we thought about the chief economist's comment, the more we realized something else was afoot. His own bank apparently did have pockets deep enough to buy the best advice which would help it avoid any regulations. But other, smaller, banks or clients might not. This can only mean two things. First, avoidance is a source of competitive advantage. Second, selling avoidance services could itself be a source of profits – large profits. Profits can be made not only, as we are often taught, despite those regulations and taxation, but in fact *out* of them. Regulatory avoidance is always good business. The more regulations are imposed, the more business opportunities are there. The more complex the regulations, the higher the fees charged for regulatory advice. This way or that, sabotaging rules and regulations is big business. So big in fact that it has become probably the single biggest source of profits for some of the largest banking houses in the world.

Let us turn, therefore, to the lucrative business of sabotaging governments.

10

THE BIG

Too-Big-to-Fail (and Jail) Banking

'US financial power would be diminished if it were left to Baby JP Morgans to compete with emerging Chinese megabanks,' warned Jamie Dimon, the CEO of J. P. Morgan, in early 2015 as he was forced to defend the bank against a potential breakup.[1]

Mr Mustier, the CEO of Italy's UniCredit, seems to share the concern about size: 'There are only two pan-European banks in Europe: BNP Paribas, present in France, Italy and Benelux, and UniCredit, present in Italy, Germany and Austria...So we have a problem...we need to have more pan-European banks, bigger banks...to support the economy.'[2]

'There is no debate – the country needs bigger and stronger banks. Therefore the consolidation of financial institutions... will be beneficial for the stability of the financial sector in the long term and for the country', argues Dinesh Weerakkody, the chairman of Hatton National Bank (HNB) in Sri Lanka.[3]

Are these the voices of concerned citizens, eager to defend their respective countries and financial institutions from vicious international competition? Not so, argue some economists. These CEOs are using their considerable rhetorical skills to defend a very lucrative portion of their business: namely, the chance to be too big to fail (known as TBTF).

TBTF is a classic sabotaging technique. Considering that the welfare of the entire nation depends on its banking institutions, if one bank becomes just big enough to the point that governments or, rather, the markets, believe that the state cannot afford to allow the bank to fail, such banks are able to borrow in the markets at lower rates. Or they may be in a position to take extra risks with their business without penalty (and presumably reap extra profits from those risky investments). The perception that a bank has become too big to fail is monetized, and becomes a great source of profit. In effect, TBTF banks enjoy an implicit subsidy from taxpayers. They enlist governments as partners, whether or not those governments agree to the deal, and buy themselves an insurance scheme on the cheap.

This theoretical premise had become much more of a reality for the academic and regulatory community in the mid-1980s, when the US authorities decided to bail out Continental Illinois, the seventh-largest US bank at the time. Subsequently one study found that following the bailout and the admission by the US Comptroller General that eleven such banks existed in the US, those eleven banks gained on average 1.3 per cent to their share value.[4] Others have shown that those eleven banks were able to issue bonds at more favourable rates compared to other banks.[5]

The monetary effects of TBTF banking are staggering. One study for the Dutch central bank estimates that TBTF subsidy in 2011 was the equivalent of 1 per cent of the GDP of Germany,

France, UK and the Netherlands. That amounted to about $100bn of subsidy per year. Andy Haldane, the chief economist of the Bank of England, believes that UK banks received annually about £100bn in subsidy as well.[6] Others have estimated that TBTF subsidy accounted for around 15 per cent of overall profitability of TBTF banks, whereas some placed the upper estimates of the subsidy as high as 50 per cent of these banks' profits.[7]

In 2008 the decision not to bail out Lehman Brothers – a comparatively small institution that was not even in the list of the top fifty banks in the world – threatened the viability of the entire North Atlantic capitalist system. It became obvious that even banks of modest size need to be carefully 'wound down' and cannot be allowed simply to fail.[8] Not surprisingly, the crisis spurred renewed interest in the question of how banks benefit from a close relationship with the state. Several studies attempted to provide estimates of the amount of subsidy enjoyed by such banks. It transpired that the 'subsidy' was generated in the markets, and thus relied entirely on market perception of (a) the point at which a bank or financial institution becomes TBTF and (b) the ability of government to bail out such bank. When such a point was reached, banks were able to borrow in the financial markets or issue bonds at lower rates than their competitors. The source of gains was twofold. On the one hand, the benefits were extended to holders of TBTF banks' debt; shareholders could benefit too. On the other hand, tertiary costs stemming from inefficient and ineffective governance structure of too big and unruly banks could be socialized.

There are other kinds of financial support that banks are structurally positioned to gain from the state. A report by the Congressional Research Service (CRS), released in late 2017 in the US under pressure from Senator Bernie Sanders, details the extent to which America's largest banks have benefited from the de facto 'free money' supplied by the Federal Reserve during the meltdown. Altogether, the Fed lent more than $3tn to financial institutions, on very generous terms, in exchange for taxpayer-backed loans; junk-rated securities were pledged as collateral. As part of one Fed programme, on thirty-three separate occasions, nine firms were able to borrow between $5.2bn and $6.2bn in US government securities for four-week intervals, paying one-time fees that amounted to the rate of 0.0078 per cent. In another, financial firms pledged more than $1.3tn in junk-rated securities to the Fed for cheap overnight loans. The rates were as low as 0.5 per cent. During one period, J. P. Morgan Chase, the second-largest bank in the US, increased its holdings of taxpayer-backed federal debt by $20bn, which yielded 2.1 per cent, while at the same time borrowing $29bn from the Fed at a rate of 0.3 per cent.

During a different three-month period in 2009, Bank of America (BoA) borrowed more than $48bn at rates ranging from 0.25 to 0.5 per cent. Meanwhile, the largest US lender tripled its holdings of Treasuries and other taxpayer-backed debt to about $15bn – securities that yielded 3.5 per cent. In the third quarter of 2009, BoA borrowed $2.9bn from the Fed through a programme that charged a mere 0.25 per cent interest. In that same period, the bank increased its holdings of taxpayer-backed federal debt by $12bn. Those securities yielded an average of 3.2 per cent.[9] In other words, BoA enjoyed a massive subsidy from the state. Was it worth it?

The 'Bank of America provided vital support to the economy throughout the financial crisis and we continue to support businesses and individuals today through our lending and capital raising activities,' explained its spokesman, Jerry Dubrowski, said to the *Huffington Post* journalist when those figures were revealed. The Fed data shows that in 2009 outstanding credit to US households declined by $234.5bn; for non-corporate businesses, credit plunged by $296.1bn.[10]

The reader is entitled to ask, then:

1. Do banks go out of their way to become too big to fail to take advantage of those subsidies?
2. If so, does their action amount to a form of sabotaging governments?

The answer to the first question is not straightforward. As we discussed in previous chapters, the management of banks such as RBS, Deutsche or Santander was hell-bent on increasing the size of their portfolios. The largest US banks expanded rapidly during the 1970s and 1980s, with the number of banks in the post-1945 US peaking in 1984. The last few decades have been marked by a decline in the number of banks, paralleled by the continued rise in the size of the assets held by the largest banks. In 2001 the five largest commercial banks held 30 per cent of total US banking system assets, topped by Bank of America, which had $552bn of assets. In 2011 the five largest banks held 48 per cent of total system assets. Four banks had total assets in excess of $1tn, and the largest commercial bank – J. P. Morgan Chase – had $1.8tn of assets, equal to 14 per cent of the total assets of all US commercial banks.[11]

But even if the trend is apparent, the reasons for expansion and mergers are not entirely clear. The banks themselves tend to justify their action in terms of optimization of costs and better services. 'Large banks invest billions of dollars to deliver the products and services consumers want – investments that only a company that has achieved scale can make. Scale allows them to deliver, like big-box stores, more innovation, greater convenience and consistent, reliable service, argued in 2012 William B. Harrison Jr, an architect of the 2000 merger that created J. P. Morgan Chase, and the bank's former chairman and chief executive.[12]

Economists tend to deduce motivation from the resulting data. Which is no proof at all. Some would like to argue, for instance, that evidence for cost reductions following a merger proves that mergers were driven by cost reduction logic. One study examined the motivation behind the merger and acquisition waves in American banking in the 1990s and concluded against the subsidy theory.[13] A different study reached the opposite conclusion: in eight mergers between 1991 and 2004 US banks have paid at least $14bn in added merger premiums in order, the authors suspect, to gain from the TBTF subsidy.[14]

It also appears that the catastrophic impact of TBTF exposed during the financial crisis only spurred banks to increase their size. J. P. Morgan exploited the turmoil to pick up Bear Stearns and Washington Mutual. Bank of America took over Merrill Lynch, the third-largest investment bank, and Countrywide Financial, the largest mortgage originator. Wells Fargo picked up Wachovia, the fourth-largest bank holding company at the time. In Europe, Santander acquired Alliance & Leicester; UK's Nationwide picked up a few smaller building societies; Barclays and Nomura sliced up the leftovers of Lehman; BNP Paribas split Fortis with the Dutch government; ING got bits of Iceland's Kaupthing. Others were taken over by governments.

Perhaps the power balance between the state and big finance is best illustrated by the post-crisis developments. On the one hand, the governments of most OECD countries have made it quite clear in the wake of the 2007–9 crisis that they are not in favour of the implicit partnership between TBTF banking and themselves. The IMF, the Financial Stability Board (FSB) and all the largest economies have introduced regulations intended to discourage banks from becoming too big to fail.

However, ten years after the crisis, regulators seem to have had a change of heart. Some are now encouraging further consolidation and growth in bank size. 'The [European) banking union has paved the way for cross-border mergers,' Danièle Nouy, chair of the ECB's Supervisory Board, declared in September 2017.[15] 'All that's missing is brave banks that will set sail to explore and conquer this new territory.' The usual arguments are invoked in support of what will become in effect TBTF, including that bigger European banks 'will be in a better position to compete with American and Asian rivals'.[16] We agree entirely with this argument. Bigger European banks will indeed be in a better position to compete internationally. They will have a new partner subsidizing them – the EU.

This may just provide an answer to our second question. The academic literature generally, and financial literature specifically, is sceptical of the quantifiable benefits of mergers and acquisitions.[17] In fact, there is solid evidence to show that most M&As in industry and in banking do not achieve the stated effects of cost-cutting and increased efficiency. So why do it? Being TBTF seems to bring an additional little bonus, the cherry on the cake. It is known as the 'Arthur Andersen effect'. In plain English, it is the phenomenon of being not only too big to fail but also too big to jail.

'Prosecuting the bank could result in a global financial disaster': so decided the leadership of the US Justice Department in 2016 – against its own internal recommendation – when there was a tangible opportunity to criminally prosecute senior HSBC executives for the bank's role in laundering some $900m of drug money and processing transactions for countries under international financial sanctions. HSBC and its American subsidiary, HSBC Bank USA, agreed to pay almost $2bn under the settlement, a deferred prosecution arrangement. Under such deals, the government agrees to delay or forgo prosecution of a company if it promises to change its behaviour.[18] The trick of the deal is that under its conditions the bank does not deny or admit guilt. It simply pays.

The 'global financial disaster' refers to the so-called Arthur Andersen effect of prosecuting a systemically sized company. The term goes back to 2002, when Arthur Andersen LLP, one of the (then) five accounting giants, was found guilty of obstruction of justice in the case of the Enron accounting fraud. Although three years later the Supreme Court would reverse the decision, that verdict had a knock-on effect on several smaller accounting firms and consultancies, leading to further scandals in the accounting industry. The WorldCom fraud and its eventual bankruptcy would become the largest implosion in that particular domino chain.

Size, therefore, whether actual or perceived, helps. Large institutional presence helps generate economies of scale and scope in banking. If growing to be considered TBTF might generate between 15 and 50 per cent of a group's profits, then very few banks can resist the temptation. Enlisting governments as your insurance policy, even against governments' will – or sabotaging your own government – has been and will remain a core strategy of banking.

The last word on this may well belong to Andy Haldane. Observing that TBTF banking is still alive and kicking, he also noted that another financial industry has been consolidating lately:

the rapidly expanding asset management sector. In this sector certain groups, such as BlackRock, Fidelity, Allianz or AXA, have grown into gigantic organizations that cannot be allowed to go down. They are, Haldane argues, the new too-big-to-fail institutions.[19]

11

———

THE BAD

Derivatives, Tax Avoidance and Evasion

Governments have become unwilling – for the most part – suppliers of insurance guarantees for large banking institutions. Not only have central banks in advanced capitalism become the classical lenders of last resort, but they had to step in as dealers of last resort, new owners and market makers for private financial institutions. When such institutions fail, the costs of the failure tend to be socialized. Society, in turn, seeks to regulate the financial system to avoid those disasters which would force it to pick up the bill, and tax the banks and their clients in order to fund costly public liabilities, including the implicit insurance for TBTF.

But these regulations and taxation can be sabotaged too. When they are sabotaged, they can become another big ticket profitability item. We do not refer to the well-known and increasingly discussed practice of tax avoidance (or 'tax planning' if you wish), aimed at reducing post-tax liabilities of the banking institutions. We refer instead to the development and innovation of a myriad of sophisticated techniques of tax avoidance as a source of business and profit. Specifically, we focus on a set of instruments that make possible profiteering from tax avoidance by offering complex financial structures to clients.

Warren Buffett famously called derivatives 'weapons of mass destruction'. Back in 2002 few understood what Buffett was on about. Today we know that he was right on the money: derivatives and other exotic financial products help conceal and amplify risk, and they can do so on a vast, system-wide scale. What is less often noted, however, is that derivatives have become weapons of sabotaging governments as well. Financial derivatives have emerged as the very heart of schemes of tax avoidance, legal chicanery and financial secrecy havens.

A financial derivative is a contract that is based on the value of the underlying asset. The underlying asset can be anything – stocks and bonds, interest rate volatility or even a natural disaster. Historically, such contracts evolved for practical and sound reasons. A European car company, for instance, sells cars in the United States. The company would need to price its cars in dollars, but its costs of production are denominated in euros. If the value of the dollar rises vis-à-vis the euro, the company gains. But if the opposite happens, the car company may end up selling cars in the US at a great loss. The company can come to an agreement with a bank or another financial institution for the purchase of dollars (or, more often, for an option to purchase dollars) at a certain predetermined rate in, say, two years' time. If the dollar falls in the meantime, the car company would still be making profits because it hedged against the fall in the dollar. The car company hedged its currency risk by buying an 'option' – a contract that gives its holder the right to buy a particular asset at a specific price in the future.

Such contracts clearly are essential instruments in today's business planning. It is estimated that about 80 per cent of global trade is intra-firm trade. It is necessary for such firms to hedge against currency, interest rates and commodity price fluctuations. Partly as a response to the varied needs of global businesses, a large secondary derivatives market has emerged, whereby derivative contracts are traded with third parties. The value of outstanding financial derivatives is more than US$500tn. Some estimates put the overall size of the derivatives market at over $1.2 quadrillion. Interest rate derivatives comprise more than 90 per cent of all contracts.

Derivatives are purchased for the flexibility they offer (parties can buy or sell in the future, but are not obliged to) and protection from changes in the market conditions (the price is pre-specified in the contract). But particular types of derivatives can provide something else. Having an option on an asset allows its holder to dissociate the ownership of the actual asset from the ownership of the options, something that most systems of taxation have not come to grips with as yet. The problem is simple.

Say, you, the reader, were lucky enough to have bought one million Apple shares in the US stock market in 1996. Since then they have appreciated tremendously. As a result, not only have you paid tax when you bought those shares, but you will have to pay capital gains tax when you sell those shares. But imagine that you were a tad more sophisticated in 1996. You are not interested in owning part of Apple. You had no intention, for example, of attending the annual shareholder meeting. What you are really after is the appreciation in the value of Apple shares. So instead of buying Apple shares, you bought a derivative contract based on Apple shares. The contract was between two parties 'betting' on the value of Apple shares in the future – which is what most 'investors' are after in any case. No share needed to be bought or sold. The derivative contract merely refers to an underlying asset, Apple shares, but has no direct link to those shares. In this case, no duty was paid on the purchase of the shares.

Let us play this scenario a bit further. Imagine that this particular contract was executed not in the US or EU, but in the Cayman Islands, a small Caribbean British overseas territory that levies no corporate taxation, no capital gains tax, or any other tax that could be remotely associated with this contract.[1] By doing so, not only have you avoided the small duty imposed on buying the shares – because, remember, you did not buy the shares. You have also avoided the capital gains or corporate tax that would accrue had you made a profit from the deal because you did not make a profit in the US. The profit was made in the Cayman Islands, which happens to levy no capital gains tax.

With a derivative contract one can bet on underlying values, in this case Apple's shares, but in a location of one's choosing. Luckily for our imaginary derivatives contractor, the Caymans have been quite generous in helping potential clients. The country has set up a Commodities & Derivatives Park for companies that undertake financial services activities directly or indirectly related to commodities, derivatives, futures and options. The park can be used by fund and investment managers to prop up trading accounts. The park even has physical electronic marketplaces for the buying and selling of stocks, stock options, bonds or commodity contracts. Perhaps it is not surprising, then, that this small island, with about 55,000 inhabitants (half of whom are expats) has emerged as the fourth- or fifth-largest financial centre in the world, on a par with Frankfurt.[2]

Everyone seems to gain from the businesses: the two parties to the contract are clearly happy they have avoided paying potential corporate and capital gains tax. The bankers who set up the deal are happy for the business and commission they have made on the deal. The Cayman Islands government is happy for attracting such value-added business into its territory. The only ones that lose from the deal are the countries and governments in which the two parties to the contract live. These countries need those taxes to maintain the security, infrastructure and economic stability that afforded the individuals or companies living there the wealth to purchase such contracts in the first place. But they have been sabotaged.

In fact, in banking and finance, taxation, regulations and 'red tape' – anything that governments impose on business or individuals in the name of maintaining the state or ensuring financial stability – can be a source of extra income. Deep in the channels of the financial system, a series of targeted and very specialized legal manipulations build into a process by which the state is being sabotaged. Yet when things go awry, as in 2007–9, when those 'weapons of mass destruction' imploded, the same banks and financial institutions did not run to the governments of the Caymans, Bermuda or Jersey for help. The banks turned to the very governments whose taxes and regulations they had helped to sabotage. In 2009 the Cayman Islands itself had to turn to the UK for a $39m bailout to plug a hole in its own budget, as the country was days away from not being able to pay its own civil servants.[3]

The Bad

. . . AND ANOTHER DERIVATIVE STORY

One need not venture offshore to avoid taxation. There are enough loopholes, ambiguities and ways of sabotaging the state to make extra profits onshore. One example of such practices is known as a basket option – a derivative contract based on a selection of different types of assets. What follows below is largely based on a scrupulous investigation by the US Congress of two major banks – Barclays and Deutsche Bank – setting up and conducting elaborate tax avoidance schemes from the late 1990s through to at least 2013, and rendering them a source of profit.

An option, as we mentioned above, is a contract that gives its holder the right to buy or sell an underlying asset at a specific price, on or before a certain date, which is precisely what our European car company in the example above bought when it 'hedged' against the volatility of a euro–dollar exchange. A basket option, however, is more complex: it involves not one asset (e.g. the dollar), but a group, or 'basket', of assets, which can include commodities, securities or currencies. Deutsche and Barclays came across an opportunity to use such baskets to sabotage financial reporting, and tax rules and regulations, and generate premium business with juicy profits (and bonuses) to boot.

How did they do it?

For a good many reasons discussed at length in the financial literature and the media, like many other countries the US government prefers longer-term investments over short-term speculations. The US has imposed, therefore, certain rules which specify that profits from investments held for less than a year are taxed at a rate of 39.6 per cent. Trades held for more than a year, on the other hand, are treated as long-term capital investment and are charged at a maximum rate of 20 per cent. A number of successful hedge funds, however, make their money from high-frequency trading, a core business model, and as such would be taxed (or their clients would be) at the higher rate (typically, as the highest tax bracket, which was 39.6 per cent before the Trump tax cuts. In the US, Deutsche and Barclays came to the rescue of those hedge funds and their clients, creating a semblance that those high-frequency trades were longer-term capital gains, subject to the lower capital gains tax.

Deutsche Bank developed and marketed a scheme it named 'Managed Account Product Structure' (MAPS). At Barclays a similar scheme went by the acronym COLT. Under this scheme the two banks would hire the hedge fund to oversee a portfolio or a basket of share options. The hedge fund, in turn, bought a two-year option linked to the portfolio. In reality, the portfolios were completely controlled by the hedge funds, and were traded very frequently. But these transactions were not taxed as short-term trades because the bank did not make profit out of them. The bank sold an option on the basket to the hedge funds, and hence it was the hedge funds that made the profit – a good profit. But the funds did not pay the 39.6 per cent tax on their profitable trading either. Strictly, they only held 'options' on the entire baskets, and they held those options for at least two years (rarely, it turned out, a day or two more than two years). The resulting profits from short-term trading were presented as long-term capital gains, which were subject to a 20 per cent tax rate (previously 15 per cent), rather than the ordinary income tax rate (39 per cent) that would otherwise apply to investors in hedge funds engaged in daily trading.

It was a sham. The US congressional committee (the Levin committee) found that often the overall composition of the securities basket changed on a second-to-second basis. One basket option account reviewed by the Securities and Exchange Commission (SEC) was found to have executed 129 million orders in a year.[4] These were clearly short-term trades. The schemes marketed by Deutsche and Barclays had no other purpose but to sabotage the regulations on short-term trading.

The scale of the business was impressive. From 1998 to 2013 Deutsche Bank AG and Barclays Plc sold 199 basket options to hedge funds, which conducted, in turn, more than $100bn in trades. One hedge fund, RenTec, which purchased a total of twenty-nine basket options with terms exceeding one year from Deutsche Bank, generated about $34bn in trading profits. An SEC examination estimated that between April 2003 and October 2007 five hedge funds utilizing MAPS options, including RenTec, had 'saved a total of $779m in taxes by exercising the option after one year'.[5] Another SEC examination report on the Barclays COLT option, used by RenTec as well, led to the deferral of $140m of taxes over a five-year period from 2002 to 2007.[6]

The banks did well out of the business, charging hedge fund fees for the financing, trading and other services. They also loaned the hedge funds the money to finance their trading in what was in the banks' proprietary accounts and reaped the resulting income. RenTec alone generated more than $1bn in financing and trading fees for Deutsche and Barclays. The US Senate report concluded that the scheme was an arrangement that 'makes no economic sense outside of an effort to bypass federal taxes and leverage limits'. In reality, the 'option' functioned as little more than a fictional derivative, permitting the hedge fund to cast short-term profits as long-term capital gains and skirt regulations on legal limits for a customer's US brokerage account.[7]

SABOTAGE

Anybody can create money, the problem is to get it accepted.

Hyman Minsky

Tax evasion and avoidance are big business, and finance is there to help. There has been a lot of talk lately about the role of tax haven jurisdictions; professional, legal and accounting advisers; and other secrecy spaces in facilitating tax avoidance. It is an important debate that needs to be had. There is one thing that is easily forgotten, however: a financial transaction in and out of low-tax jurisdiction does not take the form of gold coins hidden in the pockets of some pirates or buried in a far-flung hideout. No. All financial transactions are conducted through the infrastructure that the banks have constructed and maintain around the world. Belatedly regulators have begun to clamp down on the banking system. In 2010 the US introduced the Foreign Account Tax Compliance Act (FATCA), forcing banks to ensure that anyone trading with a US entity reveals information on their financial whereabouts. To date, FATCA has been widely seen as the most far-reaching measure targeting financial secrecy and illicit finance.

But, in finance, just when one avenue seems to be closing down, another springs into the vacant space. And while banks have had to dedicate more resources to compliance and transparency after 2007–9, demand for tax avoidance and money laundering has not subsided. Let us take a look, then, at today's dazzling new universe of cryptocurrencies that are being mined out of a computer algorithm. Or the industry of *fintech*.

12

—

THE CRYPTO

Mining the Money

'I will now buy boots for the missus!' declares a scruffy but glowing Lyonya Golubkov in the first instalment of TV commercials on Russian TV for the MMM investment company back in 1990. In the next episode he buys a fur coat for his wife. In the third Lyonya shows an upward-sloping curve illustrating the trajectory of his shrewd investment, from footwear to furniture and, finally, an apartment.

The MMM investment company grew and thrived in Russia between 1991 and 1994. In 1994 the Russian government declared the MMM securities unlawful. The company collapsed, along with the savings of up to fifteen million Russians. Sergei Mavrodi, the scheme's architect, was arrested and put in prison for tax evasion.[1] The Russian public learned a new term: Ponzi pyramid.

MMM is relevant to our story of sabotage for three good reasons. First, in any environment characterized by lax or poor regulations, like the one that thrived in 1990s Russia transitioning from planned economy to capitalism, someone is bound to take advantage of gullible people with the promise of easy money and new technology. Second, such an environment exists right now, not only in Russia but everywhere. It is the regulatory niche in which a myriad of new financial instruments and innovations, the so-called financial technology, or fintech for short, is operating.

Third, to furnish proof of concept, in 2011 the very same Sergei Mavrovi would launch a new shiny fintech version of MMM Global, now a web-based financial network promising 30–75 per cent monthly return at no risk. The network created its own virtual currency called – wait for it – the *mavro*. By 2012 the network was said to have grown to thirty-five million members worldwide in more than 100 countries, the majority of which are emerging economies. In the summer of 2018 Sergei Mavrodi unexpectedly died in Moscow. Due to the 'untimely passing of the founder, the payment of the MMM dividends cannot be made', the site announced. The MMM Global 'investors' – if that is what they were – were left holding exactly what they bought, the virtual *mavros*. It appears that they will hold those till eternity.[2]

THE FINTECH SECTOR

Fintech is a technology-anchored universe that involves, among other things, cryptocurrencies, blockchain, data mining, peer-to-peer lending, crowdfunding, money transfer services and smart contracts. Many of the innovations extend beyond financial services, where they have facilitated a range of new fundraising and investment opportunities on various platforms in cyber-space. The evolution of fintech has been both rapid and diverse, and it is clear that it can develop in any imaginable and, as yet, unimaginable direction.

Broadly, fintech is seen as a positive development. Mark Carney, the governor of the Bank of England, recognized fintech's 'huge potential for making the financial system more inclusive, efficient, effective and resilient'.[3] In March 2018 the European Commission adopted an action plan on fintech to foster a more competitive and innovative European financial sector.[4] The Fed is embracing fintech, too, although with some apprehension.

So is fintech really one of the greatest sets of innovations in finance, about to democratize the system and finally break through the strong grip that big money and big banks have on society? Not so, says Izabella Kaminska of the *Financial Times*, a sceptic. She believes that fintech is nothing but the Eurodollar market 2.0.[5] It combines many elements, from encrypted trans-actions to hidden identities and e-wallets, each of which seems to be perfectly geared to allow crime and tax evasion.

We happen to think that Kaminska is on the right track. Back in the late 1950s the niche for unregulated financial transactions in London enabled banks around the world to sabotage existing rules on capital flows, reserves, currency rates and many other national regulations. Over time the market would evolve to become the thriving financial centre in the City of London of to-day, firmly wedded to the web of former British colonies turned financial havens. While some markets centred in London have achieved great efficiencies in terms of liquidity and scale (for instance, in foreign exchange trading), the network of city-based financial institutions, as well as law and accounting firms, has been essential to making possible schemes that play a key role in regulatory arbitrage, tax avoidance and money laundering.

Cryptocurrencies have the potential to become 'super tax havens'.[6] In fact evidence suggests that they already are. To date there exist no effective enforcement mechanisms to track the online movement of bitcoins or other cryptocurrencies. According to one estimate, if even 1 per cent of funds currently sitting in offshore accounts were transferred into bitcoin, the value of this virtual currency would grow exponentially. Since the number of bitcoins in circulation is currently capped at twenty-one million, if these billions of offshore dollars migrate to that cryptocurrency, the worth of a single bitcoin could rise to nearly $3m.[7]

E-wallets exist in no physical location, are not subject to taxation at the source, and do not require the assistance of expensive financial intermediaries such as Mossack Fonseca to administer. Peer-to-peer lending lends itself directly to abuse of clients, whereas blockchain is a versatile technology. Combining several innovations in one vast cyber network, Facebook is currently trying to launch its own currency, to be called the Libra. If financial innovation normally leads to some sort of sabotage, then fintech is emerging as its Holy Grail.

REAL PROBLEMS, REAL SOLUTIONS AND SABOTAGE

Many aspects of fintech are designed to respond to real issues. Let us take the case of peer-to-peer lending. Traditionally, banks would intermediate between savers and borrowers, at a cost. And our banks, as we have learned, can be rather greedy: they impose direct costs, and then indirect fees as well, and often cheat their customers on top of that. Would it not be great to take out the middleman? Everyone wants to buy directly from the producer, and avoid paying for exorbitant dealmakers. So we try and buy from the wholesalers. We purchase our mobile phone from Carphone Warehouse, our stationery from Home Depot and our furniture from Furniture Village. Why can't we cut out the middleman in finance too?

The banks are unwittingly helping the process. During the crisis we learned just how systemic the sabotage of customers had been. After the crisis many banks gave savers 0.25 per cent or even 0.1 per cent interest on their savings (with inflation running at 1 per cent or more), and they charged borrowers much more. Worse, due to a combination of reasons, including the unintended consequences of regulations, the big banks have more or less given up on a whole segment of the economy. Small businesses, for instance, are rarely given an overdraft nowadays; and if they are, it is extended at a very high fee. The world of work has changed a lot in the past decade. Although the traditional safe and secure jobs are declining, the banks are refusing to move with the times. In a cyber universe of instant decisions and products, banks appear decidedly old-fashioned and slow-moving, with their expensive offices, mountains of paperwork and endless checks.

In the US, peer-to-peer (P2P) lending arrived in 2006, offering an alternative to traditional banks for both borrowers and lenders. It quickly established a reputation as a 'progressive consumer finance innovation' and received a further boost from the crisis of 2007–9. No longer trusting the banks (or, alternatively, being deemed too risky to be 'banked'), consumers, budding entrepreneurs and social activists have turned to new technologies to help raise funds by directly connecting savers with borrowers.

Peer-to-peer lending and crowdfunding became the direct outcomes of the fusion between technology and demands for capital. The sector has expanded and helped many good causes. By early 2018 the transaction value in the US crowdfunding segment alone was reported to have reached more than $1bn,[8] still small compared to traditional banking, but it is the fastest-growing sector.

As it is often the case with financial innovation, in an unregulated environment a good idea can turn into regulatory avoidance and sheer fraud. Many P2P firms have struggled recently with various problems. And things could get worse, warn Fed researchers following a thorough analysis of credit bureau data on 90,000 people who took out P2P loans between 2007 and 2012. Compared to ten million traditional borrowers, P2P loans do not achieve their supposed outcome. In fact, the study found, they closely resemble predatory or subprime loans, in terms of both who takes them out and the impact on borrowers' finances.[9]

Let us take a look at LendingClub, the world's largest peer-to-peer lending platform, according to Wikipedia. LendingClub enables borrowers to create unsecured personal loans ranging between $1,000 and $40,000. Investors can search and browse the loan listings on LendingClub's website and select loans that they want to invest in based on the information supplied about the borrower, amount of loan, loan grade and loan purpose. Investors make money from the interest. LendingClub makes money by charging borrowers an origination fee and investors a service fee.[10]

Clearly, an outfit like LendingClub can only survive any length of time based on its reputation – and so, one would think, it would make sure that reputation remained untainted. Not so. In 2016 LendingClub hit the headlines with a spate of all-too-familiar-sounding scandals. As it would turn out, Lending-Club mis-sold some $22m of subprime loans to a single investor against that investor's expressed conditions. An internal investigation launched by the company discovered that some staff knew the loans did not meet the investor's criteria, and that the application date on $3m of those loans had been altered to make them comply.[11] But those people seem to have chosen bonuses over clients. In April 2016 LendingClub repurchased these loans at par and subsequently resold them to another investor. That same month the company's CEO, Renuad Laplanche, resigned, and some staff were fired.

Laplanche is an interesting character. Very much like Milken, Ranieri and Masters before him, he is regarded as the godfather of the industry. It was partly his vision and innovation that led the development of P2P lending. But more revelations about this pioneer are not promising. In 2016 another investigation found that Laplanche and three of his family members took out loans from LendingClub in December 2009, just months before the company announced a major capital raising from outside investors. As loan volumes are a key metric for investors to determine online lenders' value, in effect Laplanche used the borrowings to boost the company's reported volumes for the month. In 2016 LendingClub itself reported that one of its subsidiaries failed to follow accounting standards when valuing loans. It promised to reimburse $800,000 to affected investors.[12]

In 2018 the Federal Trade Commission (FTC) charged the LendingClub Corporation with falsely promising consumers loans with 'no hidden fees'. The company deducted hundreds or even thousands of dollars in hidden upfront fees from the loans. According to the FTC, LendingClub ignored these and other warnings and, over time, made its deceptive 'no hidden fees' claim even more prominent. The FTC also alleges that LendingClub falsely told loan applicants that 'Investors Have Backed Your Loan' while knowing that many of them would never get a loan, a practice that delayed applicants from seeking loans elsewhere. In addition, in numerous instances, LendingClub has withdrawn double payments from consumers' accounts and has continued to charge those who cancelled automatic payments or paid off their loans. As a result, consumers faced overdraft fees and were prevented from making other payments. LendingClub also failed to get consumers' acknowledgement of its information-sharing policy as required by law. LendingClub was charged with violating the FTC Act and the Gramm–Leach–Bliley Act.[13]

'This is a very isolated event,' insiders would say about Lending Club in 2016. 'It should not be regarded as a mark of the industry as a whole,' others would echo. 'We do have the technology to make sure our standards are high and dealings are transparent,' repeat enthusiasts. Yet across the world in China, the $190bn peer-to-peer lending industry is a growing headache for the authorities. Hundreds of online lending platforms in China have increasingly experienced 'problems', according to Online Lending House, a research group that tracks the industry. 'Problems', in turn, range from investors being unable to withdraw money, a police investigation into a platform, or owners vanishing into thin air. These and other cases of fraud across China's shadow banking industry have prompted a broader crackdown on debt and financial risk by the authorities, partly driven by the desire to avoid expensive bailouts, as a number of China's wealth management firms, many of which are Ponzi schemes, fold.[14]

The Crypto

BLOCKCHAIN

If peer-to-peer is engulfed in scandals, what about blockchain and its most famous cyber offspring, bitcoin? Cryptocurrencies like bitcoin show the truism of Hyman Minsky's theory. Minsky, one of the greatest financial economists of the twentieth century, once said: 'Anybody can create money, the problem is to get it accepted.' Bitcoin is a currency that virtualizes in cyberspace as a reward for solving an algorithm. Bitcoin mining is an expensive business: one needs not only human capital but a lot of computer power, which in turn consumes a lot of energy. In 2013 US courts officially recognized bitcoin as a convertible decentralized virtual currency; in 2015 the Commodity Futures Trading Commission (CFTC) classified bitcoin as a commodity. Today, bitcoin can be used to pay for things and services, investors use it as an investment and there are places around the world where you can convert bitcoins into real cash; there are even derivatives on the value of bitcoin.

Bitcoin, therefore, seems to be a classic example of Minsky's theory. With blockchain and bitcoin, we do have the currency that seems to have been accepted quite widely, and the platform on which to trade it. Moreover, there are no government officials in sight, intent on padding their own pockets and building their own little bureaucratic empires. Is it not what free-market capitalism is all about?

The problem with bitcoin and other copycat cryptocurrencies, Kaminska argues, lies in the security/access paradox. 'If the sector is easily accessible (highly competitive) it's not secure, and if it's secure it's not easily accessible. Put differently, the more entrants there are, the easier it is for criminal enterprises to exploit the sector for their own ends.'[15]

And that is exactly what is happening in the cryptocurrency space. Or worse. Serious crime, such as child pornography, and drugs and arms trading, are attracted to cryptocurrencies because of its efficiency, secrecy and speed. Petty crime, like selling medicine online or ghost-writing essays for inept students, also uses crypto for secrecy.[16] Blockchain-based innovations have become the favourite method of payment in the criminal underworld. An Australian study estimated that about 47 per cent of transactions involving bitcoin are conducted on the darknet. Litecoin, the second-most-popular cryptocurrency preferred by Russians, is now accepted by nearly one-third of all dark-web vendors.[17] The industry, of course, rejects any such claims.

It gets worse. In a world where anyone can create money, crime groups have an interest in launching their own money transmission services and popularizing them as legitimate 'fintech' alternatives. As more and more jobs and services go off the official economic radar into the underground of the 'gig' economy, exchanging their skills for money, the more bitcoin and other cryptocurrencies offer a convenient way around the traditional income reporting demanded of employees and independent contractors.[18]

The authorities have taken steps to try and regulate the crypto world. The American IRS reacted to the tax implication of bitcoin use by treating it not as mere currency but as a capital asset, subject to rules governing stock and barter transactions when exchanged for dollars. Put simply, the IRS considers bitcoin a speculative investment. But for bitcoin users who prefer to trade on the black market, the IRS position is irrelevant. 'As a steroid dealer and user…I think of bitcoin as the solution to the problem of illegal tender, our so-called "paper money" economy,' says a personal trainer who accepts the cryptocurrency in payment for his pharmaceutical services. When informed that the sixteenth Amendment of the US Constitution allows the federal government to tax all income from whatever source derived, the trainer shrugged. 'I don't believe in that…I never signed or accepted the Constitution, but bitcoin is real. It's real money and it can't be stolen from me.'[19]

The IRS successfully sued Coinbase, a leading cryptocurrency exchange, to gain access to its customer records. The IRS showed the court that only 802 people reported gains or losses from Bitcoin in 2015. (The court ordered Coinbase to identify more than 14,000 customer accounts to the IRS.) In one survey of more than 2,000 American cryptocurrency owners some 57 per cent of respondents said they'd realized gains on their crypto investments, that is, profits the IRS considers taxable.[20] Fifty-nine per cent of Americans said they had never reported any such gains to the IRS.[21] Data from one popular tax preparation service shows that only a minuscule proportion – just 0.04 per cent – of US tax filers reported cryptocurrency gains or losses to the IRS in the first half of 2018. That's far fewer than the 7 per cent of Americans who are estimated to own bitcoin or another cryptocurrency, and who are likely to owe taxes to the IRS on those investments.[22]

There are several ways in which bitcoin is used for tax evasion purposes. First, bitcoin investors have gained a solid reputation for evasiveness. Some high-profile bitcoin investors have been warning their crypto compatriots to comply with IRS rules. 'When I talk to the blockchain community, I'm always pushing them – I'm like, "Dudes…pay your taxes." Because nobody in that space pays taxes,' Mike Novogratz, a billionaire hedge fund manager who now primarily invests in cryptocurrencies, said at a conference in June 2018. 'Listen, the IRS is going to come after people. People are making real money now. So the IRS isn't stupid.'[23]

Second, sabotage through crypto mirrors the general problem of financial engineering and tax evasion. Bitcoin could theoretically allow wealthy speculators to complete complicated commercial transactions, such as tax-exempt stock and gold-swapping trades that involve buying agents acting as fronts by using local currencies to facilitate the exchange. That is exactly what appears to be happening in response to the first stage of regulations concerning cryptocurrencies. The sale of bitcoin is, as mentioned above, a taxable event; but using bitcoin as *a collateral* is not. There has been a massive expansion of bitcoin-backed credit nurturing the shadow banking system. Similarly, now that bitcoin is recognized as a currency, financial derivatives based on bitcoin are also available, and those transactions are, as yet, not subject to taxation.

Speaking of derivatives and further innovations, we turn to the third facet of crypto sabotage: initial coin offerings (ICOs) and their cousin, initial token offerings (ITOs). In the cyber financial universe, ICO launches mimic an IPO of shares in a traditional stock market, except that an ICO offering is an investment in a company launching a new crypto. In a relatively unregulated environment, the range of ICO/ITO schemes appears to be limited only by their creators' imagination. A study of recent offerings classified them into several categories: 81 per cent were pure scams, ~6 per cent failed, ~5 per cent had gone dead, ~8 per cent went on to trade on an exchange.[24] In the US alone, naïve investors have drained more than $1bn into these 271 projects, with some of them still raising funds. So far, only a total of $273m has been claimed in the form of lawsuits. Since 2017 over $9bn has been raised in the form of cryptocurrencies.[25]

Faced with such challenges, the authorities are trying to protect the investors. In the US, in an almost desperate measure, the SEC launched a fake ICO. The mock website, HoweyCoins .com, represented a classic example of a fraudulent ICO website that touts an 'all too good to be true investment opportunity'. The website features the usual gimmicks, such as a misleading and blurry White Paper, guaranteed returns claims, celebrity endorsements and a countdown clock that is 'quickly running out on the deal of a lifetime'. When users click on 'Buy Coins Now', they are redirected to the website Investor.gov, which was established by the SEC to help investors avoid fraud. The site warns that if users responded to an investment offer like HoweyCoins, they 'could have been scammed'.[26]

In the UK the bank Santander had conducted a 'fake job advert' experiment to discover how many Brits would apply for a job as a money mule – an activity that helps criminals launder money. To appear alluring, the job ad drew heavily on fintech buzz. Out of 2,000 people presented with the ad, one-third said they would apply for the job; only 15 per cent rightly identified the role as that of a money mule. Of those who fell for the ad, 7 per cent said they would still apply for the job even after they were informed it was for a role as a money mule.[27]

All this may, again, be seen as a set of very isolated tests, at the dawn of a new techno age. Yet the scale of competition and the speed of development in the industry creates a structural vulnerability. Even legitimate entrants can be easily taken advantage of by groups seeking to launder funds. The more money service companies there are, the easier it is for criminal networks to spread and disguise their illicit business and/or move from one service provider to the next as they get frozen out. Since many of their strategies involve the employment of money mules, the presence of more providers makes it easier to extend the life cycle of the money mules in the system before they get detected and frozen out.

CONCLUSION

Enthusiasts of blockchain-based payment advances in finance stress the liberating aspects of these innovations, and the inevitability of technological progress. Sceptics of financial and technological innovations, and those familiar with the history of manias, panics and crashes, know that any technological boom is marked by a good portion of dubious and overtly fraudulent schemes. As with many financial instruments, the problem does not lie with fintech as such, but in the conditions of a rapidly innovating competitive financial environment that is relatively unregulated.

Inevitably, such an environment invites the saboteurs. This simple fact about the business of finance has been known, as we will see in the next chapter, for rather a long time, except that it is one of those unpleasant truths that somehow fell out of fashion. With disastrous consequences.

PART FIVE

CONCLUSION

13

———

OLD NEWS

The crisis of 2007–9 created a massive workload for governments, think tanks, international institutions, academia and courts. A lot of money and resources have been spent on parliamentary hearings, expert studies and legal proceedings inquiring into the causes of the meltdown. On both sides of the Atlantic regulatory bodies have been revamped and new institutions created, with an explicit remit to govern finance better and avoid the problems that brought on the events of 2007–9. It appears that the money was not spent in vain: a wide variety of measures and thousands of pages of new regulations were introduced and published, all aimed at mending the ills of the pre-crisis financial system. Banks were slapped with multibillion-dollar fines. A few financiers went to prison.

Yet nowhere in the thousands of pages of reports, or among the avalanche of new rules and regulations, is there a mention of sabotage as a system-wide practice in finance. While in the immediate aftermath of the crisis there were a few endeavours to focus on fostering a new 'culture' of banking and better ethics in the industry, most of these initiatives have remained vacuous. Unsavoury practices, including behaviour bordering on criminality, continue to be treated as aberrations, as random and highly unusual deviations from the otherwise stable, market-governed process of financial intermediation. Nor does the post-crisis literature dwell much on the link between competitive markets, profitability and the tactics of market control in today's finance, control that inevitably causes harm.

Not a surprise, you may think. The notion of the degrees and effects of market competition appears rather theoretical. Debating it may be appropriate in academic forums, but is likely to be a waste of time in the rather short-termist domain of policymaking. Likewise, the argument about sabotage in the financial system is, at best, provocative. How can it possibly form the basis of regulatory guidance? Well, if you do think that way, maybe it is time to think again – because the theory of sabotage does not simply have the *potential* to inform financial regulation: it once was the very foundation of the regulatory paradigm.

It was the 1930s, and the US and international economies had been shattered by the 1929 financial crisis. Reflections on practices of market sabotage in the financial system guided the great regulatory drive that would form the basis of the postwar financial architecture. The regulatory environment that was established across the advanced industrialized world is commonly remembered (and romanticized) as a system that prioritized what many consider the 'real economy' over finance, and welfare over markets. This view has become so well entrenched that the two postwar decades are sometimes referred to as the era of 'financial repression',[1] an era dominated by manufacturing and productive capital that kept speculative finance at bay.

Nostalgically, the short-lived Bretton Woods era is sometimes referred to as 'the golden age of capitalism'.

Whether or not that was a golden age, what seems to have been forgotten is that the financial regulations which kept the financial system stable were designed in the 1930s to tackle, first and foremost, the problem of sabotage head-on. It would be only in the late 1970s and onwards that those regulations intended to challenge sabotage were gradually hollowed out. Under the spell of a new, neoliberal theory of the market and politics, and through the development of alternative platforms, organizations and markets, regulators either rolled back the rules and provisions originally targeting sabotage in finance or simply sidestepped many of them.

The crisis of 2007–9 was distinct from the one that sparked the Great Depression. But due, at least partially, to the rollback of the 1930s regulations, there are some uncanny similarities between them, if not in the way the crises have been dealt with, then in the system-wide dynamics that led the financial systems to their breaking points. It may be worthwhile therefore, to understand the philosophy behind the regulatory efforts in the US in the 1930s, soon emulated all over the world.

THE PECORA REPORT OF 1934 AND FINANCIAL REGULATION

To understand the philosophy behind the new financial regulations of the 1930s, the Senate Committee on Banking and Currency investigation of the causes of the financial crisis of 1929, known as the Pecora Report,[2] is as good a starting point as any. Although Ferdinand Pecora was personally involved in many interviews with bankers and financiers during the investigation, the report did not use emotive language such as 'sabotage'. The report was intended, in the words of its authors, to expose 'banking operations and practices deemed detrimental to the public welfare;…unsavoury and unethical methods employed in the flotation and sale of securities;…[and] devices whereby income-tax liability is avoided or evaded'.[3] Pecora uncovered widespread 'abuses', and 'unsavoury' and 'unethical' behaviour all round, which 'brought in its train social consequences inimical to the public welfare'.[4] The 400 pages of text, complete with references to documents and transcripts of interviews with the high-profile financiers of the day, provide a great deal of evidence of the pervasiveness of sabotage in the financial system.

Chapter I of the Pecora Report discusses the widespread techniques of stock market manipulation. Back in the early 1930s the investigation identified 'over-the-counter' markets as an issue of great concern – these markets proved particularly amenable to techniques of sabotage, as indeed the cases discussed in this book show. The chapter surveys a litany of the 'manipulative devices' employed during the 1920s boom by financial houses intended to sabotage their clients, including 'margin purchasing', which is 'speculation in securities with borrowed money'.[5]

Ominously reminiscent of the doomed subprime markets of the 2000s, the report identifies:

The celerity with which margin transactions were arranged and the absence of any scrutiny by the broker of the personal credit of the borrower, encouraged persons in all walks of life to embark upon speculative ventures in which they were doomed by their lack of skill and experience to certain loss.[6]

It is as if, decades later, those brokers selling mortgages, soon to be securitized as MBSs, opened the Pecora Report and said to each other: 'Ah, that's the way to do this.'

The banks, the report concludes, were aware of the perils to those customers, but were more interested in a quick buck. What the banks did not factor in – just as their successors did not some seventy years later – were the systemic implications of their actions. Across the economy, the mounting loans inevitably created fragility, leading to the crash of 1929 and the Depression.

Pecora then moves on to another technique in vogue at the time, the practice of 'pooling' resources among various financial actors. Like councils of thieves, financial houses would pool their resources to influence the prices of a stock, only to dump their holdings once the market bought enough of the stock at the inflated price. Leverage and pooling were exercised not because traders were so convinced by their diagnosis and were prepared to take greater risks. No, 'The investigation has shown that the purpose of a pool generally is to raise the price of a security by concerted activity on the part of the pool members, and thereby to enable them to unload their holdings at a profit upon the public'.[7] In other words, just as RBS, Goldman and the founder of the LendingClub would do many years later, financial houses pooled their resources to create an impression that certain securities were successful, only to fleece the unsuspecting public. The chapter concludes that 'some of the methods employed by stock-exchange members to stimulate active trading were technically in conformity with stock-exchange rules and yet worked incalculable harm to the public'.[8]

The report then continues with a chapter on investment banking, noting its 'Tendency toward monopoly'.[9] There is a fine section describing 'Speculation and the investment banker'.[10] The chapter outlines how banks had their own 'preferred lists' of clients, employing 'unsound practices', including excessive compensation paid to investment bankers, '"finders'" fees', abuse stemming from the interrelationship of commercial and investment banking, voting trusts, collateral manipulations, abuse of foreign bond issues to Peru, Brazil, Chile and the like.[11]

For Pecora, 'A prolific source of evil has been the affiliated investment companies of large commercial banks.'[12] In other words, the greatest abuses arose out of the interrelationship of commercial and investment banking. Investment companies and trusts were set up to leverage control or create opacity, rather than for investment purposes.[13] The line between investment trusts and holding companies was nebulous, with the effect that the former became the latter.[14] Special investment corporations (today we call them special purpose vehicles) were often used precisely for the same purposes. Pecora notes the tendency towards 'pyramiding corporation upon corporation, investment trust upon investment trust, and holding company upon holding company'.[15] These techniques were used to circumvent the Sherman antitrust laws and generate monopolies. 'The primary motivation for the organization of the holding company has now become the development and financial promotion of security-selling schemes',[16] whereby 'intercompany accounting...rendered the financial reports incomprehensible'.[17]

Pecora's Chapter III moves on to commercial banking, pointing to a series of abuses, including securities speculations, violation of fiduciary duty to depositors, pool operations and the like, raising questions about the 'Ethics of banking officers'.[18] Private banking is subject to special scrutiny with regards to their practices. The following chapter discusses tax avoidance techniques, including avoidance by transfer of securities to relatives, tax avoidance by sale of securities through foreign corporations and tax avoidance by dissolution of partnerships at propitious intervals. Chapter VI looks at the practices of investment trusts and holding companies and concentration of control of wealth, including abuses such as concentration of control of the public's money, excessive profits to organizers, leverage through pyramidal structures of holding companies and 'uploading' of securities on investment trusts.

FINANCIAL REGULATION AFTER PECORA

In effect, the Pecora report is a detailed study of sabotage in finance. And while congressional investigations generally do not shy from apportioning blame, the purpose of Pecora, in its own words,

> has been to lay the foundation for remedial legislation in the fields explored and in some measure that purpose has already been achieved. During the progress of this investigation, Congress enacted the Banking Act of 1933, the Securities Act of 1933, the Securities Exchange Act of 1934, and several amendments to the revenue act calculated to eliminate methods of tax avoidance described before the subcommittee.[19]

What was Pecora's overall verdict? The problem with finance, the report argues, can be distilled down to six core points:

> First, the financial industry is highly conflicted, and, if allowed, is likely to abuse its clients.

Second, financial houses are leveraged to the hilt; if allowed, they will use their knowledge of the economy in an abusive manner.

Third, the bigger financial houses have tended to short-change the smaller ones.

Fourth, bankers ensure that profits are flowing to them, but if left unpunished will also ensure that their mistakes are paid for by others.

Fifth, financial houses use financial instruments for tax evasion and avoidance purposes.

Sixth, financial houses use investment funds, holding companies and the like to achieve great leverage, conceal ownership and create accounting opacity. It takes longer, therefore, for the regulator to appreciate the faltering state of finance.

The combined impact of these practices was the systemic fragility that would eventually implode in October 1929. The regulations that Pecora recommended (some put in place during the proceedings) were meant, first and foremost, to remove opportunities for abuse and sabotage in the financial system. The Banking Act of 1933, known as the Glass–Steagall Act, made amendments to the Federal Reserve Act. Key among those amendments was the separation of investment and commercial banking activities. These rules were meant to weaken banking leverage over the economy, help to lift the veil of opacity generated by the mixing of commercial and investment banking activities, and separate strategy and investment from other banking activities.

An amendment to the Federal Reserve Act required the Federal Reserve Board to supervise member banks, 'keep itself informed of the general character and amount of the loans and investments of its member banks with a view to ascertain whether undue use is being made of bank credit for the speculative carrying of or trading in securities, real estate, or commodities'. For this purpose, each bank was required to file yearly reporting on activities of all affiliates. When two or more member banks within the same Federal reserve district were affiliated with the same holding company, they were reduced to one.[20]

Still, Pecora felt that one area was not dealt with. That was the personal responsibility of bankers and the need to abide by rules of ethical behaviour. That last unaddressed point was never revisited, with consequences that we have come to appreciate some seventy years later.

So there we have it. Sabotage in the financial system is old news. But this old news was increasingly ignored and eventually forgotten. One by one the remedial legislations that were intended to tame and remove sabotaging incentives and techniques were lifted in the name of efficiency and removal of 'red tape'. Attempts to revisit the cases, address the issues and amend those rules have been sparse, overshadowed by the ideological framework supporting the new type of finance and its apparently functional role in the economy. Mirroring the evolution of the field, regulators shifted their focus from sabotage as a cause of systemic failure to the symptom of failure: namely, financial instability. As long as finance was 'stable' – that is, as long as banks did not collapse and markets appeared liquid – the financial system was considered to be in good shape.

With the growing sophistication of the financial system, regulators increasingly adopted the notion that the 'financial system' could remedy its own problems. Self-interested financial actors would balance each other and ensure that the 'market' would root out unsavoury behaviour. Financial institutions, keen to maintain credibility and market reputation, would navigate the risks prudently. It became fashionable to believe that egotism and self-interest will ensure an optimal playing field. Financial innovation has been celebrated in the name of democratizing finance, expanding credit and improving the techniques of mediating between capital markets and borrowers.

The real scandal of the costs of deregulated finance is not that it unravelled amid the financial fiasco of 2007–9. It is that its origins had been uncovered and dealt with back in the 1930s, practically to the last detail. Then, during the two decades that led up to the repeal of the Glass–Steagall Act in 1999 and certainly during the decade that followed, sabotage in finance ceased to be a regulatory concern. The behaviour itself, however, did not go away. How could it? How else, asks our friend the ex-Goldman trader, could you make money in this business?

PECORA'S SIX POINTS TODAY

So let us look closer at Pecora's key findings, in light of what we know today.

1. The financial industry is highly conflicted, and, if allowed, is likely to abuse its clients.

Today's finance thrives on conflict. One might think that the crisis of 2007–9 may have helped to address if not the underlying conflict of interests in finance, then at least its most blatant exploitations. But the conflict in finance is not only about individuals within banks; nor is it about individual banks as such. It is based on the inevitable asymmetry of power between the big and the small, between the sell and the buy side, and between the regulator and the market. In a competitive system, where profits are easily eroded by competition, size is one way to control the market. In a business that trades in estimations of future values, information – about futures sales of assets, planned mergers, hostile acquisitions – is highly sought after because it can be monetized. The bigger you are as a financial institution, the easier it is for you to monetize this information and capitalize on the power asymmetries stemming from it. And while after 2009 there has been some renewed concern about the very large banking conglomerates, now called 'systemically important financial institutions', the concern is not about knowledge or the use of information but overwhelmingly about the costs of a potential failure of a large bank.

Equally, the conflict of interest between finance and clients has not been addressed. It was well after 2009 that Wells Fargo made up over *one and a half million* fake clients and moved some of real clients' money into fictional accounts. It is well after 2009 that wealth managers trick their special clients into hidden fee structures and unneeded products. And even if you are not particularly sympathetic towards the plight of high-net-worth individuals, consider millions of customers of new lending platforms, including in the fintech sector, that promise astronomical returns to their investors, only for the new crypto managers to melt into the ether of the Internet, together with the invested funds.

It must tell us something that the Consumer Financial Protection Bureau (CFPB), created in 2010 in the US as part of the post-crisis reform, was the most difficult measure to pursue politically. It is also telling that the bureau, which could have addressed some of the tendencies towards sabotage, is one of the post-crisis institutions the Trump administration is keen to overhaul: three advisory boards have been disbanded by Trump's finance protection chief.[21] Time will tell whether or not the White House will succeed in dismantling the system of finance consumer protection altogether.

2. Financial houses are leveraged to the hilt; if allowed, they will use their knowledge of the economy in an abusive manner.

The post-crisis banking system in the UK has an average leverage of around 25:1.[22] In the US, non-financial firms have been borrowing more since 2009, while the authorities have recently relaxed the rule on leverage in the banking system. In parallel, new, 'shadow' banking institutions have expanded since 2009 across the world, and today operate across several important segments of the economy. Most of them play a function in extending the credit system; many operate with high leverage, often in ways that are poorly understood or simply invisible. Therefore, even if the banking system may be considered to be better capitalized today than it was in 2007 (a claim that remains to be tested), the non-banking parts of the financial system have continued to grow and regulation simply has not kept up with this trend. The question remains: Who will pay?

3. The bigger financial houses have tended to short-change the smaller ones.

The renewed drive for greater 'efficiency' in post-2009 finance is threatening smaller financial institutions, many of which have emerged as challengers to older banks after the crisis. Unsurprisingly, perhaps, the large banking houses are fighting back. Ten years on, banking in the US has consolidated into four or five big institutions, while in Europe the fragmented national banking systems remain vulnerable to takeovers and other risks. Further consolidation is likely and, indeed, seen by some as a solution to the European financial system's lack of competitiveness. Jamie Dimon, the legendary CEO of J. P. Morgan, has been a champion for the cause of bigger banks, applying his considerable political skills on the practical side: he lobbied hard against the introduction of Basel III capital requirements on bigger banks, which he deemed 'un-American'.[23]

4. Bankers ensure that profits are flowing to them, but if left unpunished will also ensure that their mistakes are paid for by others.

Actually, why confine yourselves to profit flows? What if you can get handsomely paid for losses, too? Let's consider a very interesting report by Andrew Cuomo, attorney general of New York, published in 2009. The report, subtitled 'Heads I Win, Tails You Lose Bank Bonus Culture', provides a detailed analysis of the size of bonuses paid out by big US banks during the 2007–9 meltdown. It notes, for instance, that

> large payouts became a cultural expectation at banks and a source of competition among the firms. For example, as Merrill Lynch's performance plummeted, the bank severed the tie between pay based on performance and set its bonus pool based on what it expected its *competitors* would do...Merrill paid out close to $16bn in 2007 while losing more than $7bn and paid close to $15bn in 2008 while facing near collapse. In 2007–08, Merrill's losses more than erased Merrill's earnings between 2003 and 2006.[24]

TABLE 13.1. [25]

TARP RECIPIENTS' 2008 BONUS CHART

Below is a chart of the original nine TARP recipients for 2008 highlighting each banks earnings/losses bonus pool, number of employees, earnings per employee, amount of TARP funds received and the amount of bonus payments in excess of $3 million, $2 million and $1 million.

	Earnings/ (Losses)	Bonus Pool	# of Employees	Earnings Employees	Bonus Employees	TARP	≥$3 M	≥$2 M	≥$1M
Bank of America	$4,000,000,000	$3,300,000,000	243,000	$16,461	$13,580	$45 B	28	65	172
Bank of New York Mellon	$1,400,000,000	$945,000,000	42,900	$32,634	$22,028	$3 B	12	22	74
Citigroup, Inc	($27,700,000,000)	$5,330,000,000	322,800	($85,812)	$16,512	$45 B	124	176	738
Goldman Sachs Group	$2,322,000,000	$4,823,358,763	30,067	$77,228	$160,420	$10 B	212	391	953
J.P. Morgan Chase & Co	$5,600,000,000	$8,693,000,000	224,961	$24,893	$38,642	$25 B	>200		1,626
Merrill Lynch	($27,600,000,000)	$3,600,000,000	59,000	($467,797)	$61,017	$10 B	149		696
Morgan Stanley	$1,707,000,000	$4,475,000,000	46,964	$36,347	$95,286	$10 B	101	189	428
State Street Corps	$1,811,000,000	$469,970,000	28,475	$63,600	$16,505	$2 B	3	8	44
Wells Fargo & Co.*	42,933,000,000	$977,500,000	281,000	($152,786)	$3,479	$25 B	7	22	62

A particularly poignant element in the report is a table, reproduced at left, which shows that the big banks that made heavy losses during the crisis (and received large sums of bailout money from the US government) also had the highest 'earnings per employee' ratios.

Academics have a name for this. They call this trend, 'socializing the risks, while privatizing profits'. Since 2007 the world central banks have pumped an estimated $9tn into the banking system, with US Fed and the Bank of Japan contributing the largest amounts.[26] The balance sheet of the world's *de facto* central bank, the Federal Reserve, has expanded from $908bn in 2008 to $4.5tn in 2018.[27] Money created through these unprecedently large government programmes was aimed at helping the economies to recover from the post-crisis recession.

Ten years on, most economists agree – an usual occurrence in the profession known for endless disagreements – that such an unprecedented expansion has missed its aim. Instead, the newly created liquidity generated asset inflation, prompting an exponential rise in real estate and equity values – and, on the back of those, rapid growth of the wealth management sector. Assets under management have grown from about $22tn in 2005 to around $80tn today (which is higher than the world's GDP). The industry of wealth management is projected to grow further, with assets being managed professionally projected to expand to $145tn by 2025. In the meantime, most crisis-hit economies had been strapped into economic austerity measures that had been pushed by governments as a solution for the legacy of the financial crisis.

5. Financial houses use financial instruments for tax evasion and avoidance purposes.

This chapter is written amid the revelations from the scandal of Danske Bank, Denmark's largest bank. In 2018 it transpired that

Danske had laundered €200bn ($235bn) of illicit Russian cash between 2007 and 2015, via its Estonian subsidiary. The bank's CEO and chief legal officer had to step down. The bank, one of Europe's most respected institutions not so long ago, now faces a criminal investigation from the US Department of Justice. As the scandal erupted, it appeared that both the Danish government and investors knew about the bank's internal suspicions and warnings as early as 2014–15, but did nothing to prevent the flow of cash.

Danske is not the first, and very likely not the last, established bank to be linked to a money-laundering and tax evasion scheme. Nordea, another respected European bank, is currently facing similar allegations. According to one of our interviewees who works in a senior position in a leading bank in the US, the expanding wealth management sector and the growth of private banking divisions in the main banks increasingly mean that today a large part of the financial system is 'banking for plutocrats'.

6. Financial houses use investment funds, holding companies and the like to achieve great leverage, conceal ownership and create accounting opacity. It takes longer, therefore, for the regulator to appreciate the faltering state of finance.

Not to go too far, let us take Ireland as an example. A country known for its emerald greenery and rain, it is also a key node in the global hub of financial engineering. In fact, Ireland is so central to international financial opacity that it lends its name to a highly-sought-after product: a double Irish sandwich.

The 'sandwich' refers to an accounting and tax scheme which allows companies to avoid taxation. Since the late 1980s it has been mostly been used by US multinationals to avoid corporate taxation on all non-US profits. Historically, Double Irish is the largest tax avoidance tool. It has enabled US companies to shield around $100bn annually from taxes. Double Irish has often been paired with the Dutch Sandwich – another tax avoidance instrument. Although the US authorities were aware of the scheme, it was the EU that in October 2014 forced Ireland to close the scheme, with effect from January 2015. As the policy was being announced, Ireland had offered replacement tools for tax avoidance, including something that is now called Single Malt – an arrangement between Ireland and Malta that allows companies to make profits in one country but be taxed in another.[28]

Ireland is also one of the world's largest hubs for SPVs – special purpose vehicles widely used in finance to restructure debt and issue securities. Ireland-based SPVs have been linked to a series of financial scams – proven and yet unproven, often involving banks and funds from emerging markets. One of the recent cases involves the International Bank of Azerbaijan (IBA), which used obscure Dublin-based entities to sell bonds. The bonds were bought by state-linked funds in Kazakhstan. Three years later the Baku-based lender defaulted, and its CEO was put in prison for embezzlement, while a $22bn national pension fund in Kazakhstan had to probe its investment in the debts. IBA, controlled by the Azeri state, has borrowed about $900m since 2007 through Dublin-based SPVs in deals arranged by J. P. Morgan and Citigroup.[29]

In 2015 five of the largest banks in the world, J. P. Morgan, Bank of America Merrill Lynch, Deutsche Bank AG, Nomura Holdings and Morgan Stanley, reported zero corporate tax in the UK, the largest international financial centre in the world. Together with Goldman Sachs and UBS, which did pay some corporate tax in the UK that year, the seven banks employed 33,000 staff in the UK, reported revenues of £20bn in the UK and profits of £3.5bn, but ended up paying a combined total of £21m in corporation tax.[30]

Meanwhile, the twenty biggest European banks posted profits of at least £18bn in global tax havens in 2016.[31] Collectively, these institutions made €4.9bn (£4.2bn) in profits in Luxembourg, more than they made in the UK, Sweden and Germany combined. Country-by-country data suggests that European banks did not pay a single euro in tax on €383m in profits made in tax havens in 2015.[32]

Like many crises before it, the global financial meltdown has been an educating experience. For instance, we know more today about how a bank may be 'wound down', or how many derivatives are traded on organized platforms, or what securitization entails. But one important question about the business of finance remains puzzling: Specifically, how are our financiers able to register superprofits so consistently?

Economic theory tells us that it is next to impossible to make money in competitive markets. Business bulletins tell us that our financiers reap huge profits, even in the face of market shifts and regulatory shocks. Financial markets are commonly assumed to be highly competitive; so how are superprofits possible? Some eighty years ago Pecora found that, inevitably, the superprofits made in finance are traceable to some form of what Veblen called 'sabotage': they stem from a form of hindering, obstructing, delaying, misrepresenting, destroying or otherwise taking advantage of the 'dumbest person in the room'.

14

SO WHAT?

We saw our task in this book as that of translators, interpreting the good work that has been and is being done by academics and the professional media investigating the dynamics of the financial sector. We spoke with people in finance, especially those able to take a broader, systemic view of the industry. We also talked to academics and customers of the financial sector, including a few high-net-worth individuals. We have learned a lot. We then decided to look back at the history of the regulation of the financial industry, starting with the Pecora Report.

We came across an intriguing dialogue that took place in 1934 between Senator Ferdinand Pecora and a certain Mr Whitney, during the investigation into a range of manipulative devices used by financiers in the run-up to the 1929 crash and subsequent depression:

> Pecora: 'And by a free and open market you do not mean a controlled market, do you?'
> Mr. Whitney: 'What is a controlled market?'[1]

This exchange probably reflects Pecora's innermost thoughts about the core problem of the business of finance. It also captures the gist of what we have learned from our study of the industry. Pecora's meticulous investigation found that under the pretence of aiming for free and open competition, financial actors sought to gain control over the markets. They did so through sabotaging a 'captured' slice of their markets by taking advantage of their clients; by undermining their competitors (by ensuring that competition does not create an even playing field), or by sabotaging governmental rules, the rules that were supposed to maintain the free and open market.

Nearly nine decades on, the mechanics of financial sabotage have changed in form, but not in substance. The question is, why is sabotage so persistent? We found two related reasons. First, neither Pecora nor we are suggesting that financial actors harm their clients, competitors or governments on purpose, for the sheer pleasure of doing so. Financial actors seek to control their markets and engage in sabotage not because they are particularly greedy or have gone rogue, but because they try and insulate themselves from the vagaries of genuine competition and from the harsh discipline of the price mechanism, which inevitably will ensure that profits are wafer-thin. The way they go about it often does inflict harm on their clients, competitors and the state.

Second, we believe that sabotaging continues unabated not least because the penalties for carrying it out are slim. The regulations that were introduced to target sabotage some eight decades ago have been 'rolled back' in the name of market efficiency and a robust financial system. In turn, the post-2009 reforms, although ostensibly comprehensive, are built on the assumption

that the market does work in 'normal' times. As such, they priori-
tize issues of market stability and crisis management.

The question is, why? Given the material discussed above,
and in light of many other studies and memoirs of ex-financiers
and regulators describing the widespread malaise in the industry, it seems rather odd that sabotage is not recognized for what
it is: a systemic feature of the financial system. Then there is an
additional puzzle as to why regulations developed and designed
to combat the market-controlling tendencies were rolled back.
The answers to these questions have their own history.

To begin with, sabotage is too impolite a term. This is what
our interviewees invariably implied. Business is important in
capitalism, and the financial system is essential to the functioning of any economy. Talking about sabotage as a systemic behavioural trait raises uncomfortable questions about the very
system we inhabit, and that is not an easy thing to do. We all are
in it together, remember?

Next, the problem goes beyond etiquette and convention. For
centuries, and due to the centrality of the City in London, and
then Wall Street in New York, the foundational legal framework
governing finance has been based on common law. In this legal
framework, it is the established business practice that precedes
and informs legal convention. This primacy of business convention, in turn, has enabled the financial industry not only to shape
the rules of the game by, for instance, advising the government
on market regulations but also to rely on legal constructs such
as limited liability to escape responsibility. This makes it more
difficult to identify those responsible: the prosecutors always
face the challenge of providing evidence of the intent and ille-
gality of an action. Even when a case against a bank is brought

to court (as, for instance, in the Abacus case), the challenge is to prove that someone specific within the institution had the intent to harm the client or business partner. The legal chicanery and financial engineering that shroud financial contracts ensure that the financial institution is well within the letter, if not the spirit, of the law. This makes prosecution a challenging, laborious and expensive process.

Finally, there are deeper, paradigmatic reasons. The main priority of financial regulation today is not to amend business conduct in an ethical direction, but to ensure the stability of the financial system. In the wake of the 2007–9 crisis, the world's central banks and financial regulators place great emphasis on the distribution of risks in the system, probabilities of institutional failure and crisis management. This is, undeniably, a good thing.

In fact, this focus on financial stability is itself a revolution: it crept on to the regulatory agenda only after the wave of crises of the late 1990s. In the heyday of the 'neoliberal era', in the 1980s and 1990s, financial stability was not a subject of consistent regulation, simply because, left to itself, it was the market that was supposed to deliver stability. In fact, up until the meltdown of 2007–9 academics and regulators had been arguing about whether central banks should concern themselves with financial stability in the first place. The crisis and its aftermath accelerated the resolution of that debate in favour of financial stability, but it is quite telling that moves towards greater transparency in finance and the introduction of new institutions of consumer protection were the most difficult among the reform measures during the post-2009 period.

When you hear bankers complain about the new costs of post-2009 regulations, do believe that they are sincere. Never in the past six decades has the banking system been so tightly regulated and watched. Compared to the pre-2007 heyday of finance, today's costs of compliance, audit and account management for banks are exorbitant. 'The balance sheet,' one senior London banker told us, 'has become a scarce resource.' International banking channels and clearing systems are used to police terrorists and money launderers. Spare some sympathy, too, for the so-called global systemically important financial institutions (SIFIs): their regulatory burden is higher still, and they are under constant scrutiny. Rule makers and regulators at national and international levels now target the banking system through a series of sophisticated and wide-ranging set of models, requirements, tests and probes.

The new regulations are developed with one idea in mind. By raising the costs of noncompliance, they intend to induce a behavioural change in the industry. The behavioural change, in turn, is thought to be needed in order to make the system more robust and stable. And who can argue with that? Surely a more robust financial system serves the 'real' economy better than a fragile one?

Alas, stability is a funny and, dare we say it, potentially a misleading term. It was Hyman Minsky, now a classic figure in finance, who quipped that stability is always destabilizing. In an environment of economic optimism about the future, dangers easily become undervalued and economic agents engage in increasingly risky activities. Ultimately, these risks materialize as unpayable debts, and a financial crisis ensues. But stability is precarious not only because it breads instability but also because it nurtures sabotage.

This brings us to a somewhat surprising set of conclusions. The business of finance can begin to work for society provided regulations target the very instinct of business to control markets. With this verdict, we take, therefore, a clear pro-market but an anti-business stance. We think that regulations in finance should be concerned, first and foremost, with the business aspect, with the attempt to sabotage the market in its broadest sense.

Are we calling for a new Pecora, then? A reintroduction of the 1930s regulations in the twenty-first century? No, at least, not in the literal sense. The financial architecture of the 1930s remains the closest analogy we have to date to an arrangement that does target sabotage. Contrary to common belief, the principal cause of and rationale for the financial regulations that Pecora proposed, including those that became the basis for the Glass–Steagall Act, were not meant to distort the markets. Fundamentally, those regulations were *pro-market, but anti-business*. They were meant to safeguard the financial market from attempts to control the flow of information and outcome by financial actors. It seems that this distinction – between the market and business – is the most difficult hurdle to be overcome when discussing financial regulation today.

The 1930s framework of financial regulation was not based on a binary distinction between the market on the one hand and regulation on the other. Senator Pecora and his fellow committee members understood business, as we described in Chapter 1, as an imposition of the pecuniary principle on every aspect of life. The Pecora Report is both lengthy and incisive. It alludes to a problem that can best be described as ideological. It appears that sabotage in finance, or the various techniques of controlling markets we have described in this book, works best under the pretence of a free market. The notion of the free market, to which all businesses in finance purportedly subscribe, is used as a perfect veil to sabotage clients, competitors or the state. It is a world of smoke and mirrors, where ideology and political debates are harnessed in support of techniques of sabotage.

The challenge of any regulation targeting sabotage in the finance of the twenty-first century is to move beyond the in-built focus on individual institutions and personalities and recognize instead that regulatory arbitrage, opacity and even innovation are the perennial means to capture and control the market. We call, therefore, for a return to the philosophy of the 1930s, the philosophy that was both pro-market but anti-business, and the philosophy that yielded policies which were intended to protect the consumers of finance from sabotage at the core of the regulatory drive.

This philosophy has been forgotten. We have become accustomed to thinking along binary tracks. The typical policy debate in finance mirrors a broader schism between the Left and the Right in politics. It is a schism between a 'pro-market' (private) and 'pro-state' (regulatory) instinct. The former camp, typically associated with the Right, advocates policies that assume the primacy of the market, and since it is seen as the most efficient technique of resource allocation, the political Right believes that the more the market functions are left unregulated and the more the state is rolled back, the freer and more efficient the market will be. As businesses are the agents of the market, this position is also called 'pro-business'.

The Left takes a different view. The Left has always been suspicious of theories or claims about market efficiency. Instead, progressive academics point out that markets inherently create winners and losers, and over time the winners use their institutional power to embed their advantage in law and institutions. A class society emerges, and so does a structural gap between the rich and the poor, which is difficult to correct within the existing system. Market scepticism was given an added boost by Keynes and his followers, many of whom equated liberalized financial markets with the freedom to speculate. A theory emerged differentiating between the 'good' and 'bad' financial trade. Good trade supports investment in the 'real' economy; bad financial trade is done purely for short-term, speculative gains.

This binary reasoning is rather simplistic, and it is indicative that a third way has emerged between these two positions. In the political aftermath of the 2007–9 financial crisis it is quite fashionable to be anti-market but pro-business. Business, we are told, creates jobs and wealth for society, whereas markets are inherently unstable: left on their own, they tend to crash. It is also quite trendy to be anti-finance, which is often seen as being 'a curse' on the rest of the economy. Both positions, we suggest, while aspiring for a fairer economy, miss an important point. In the free, transparent and competitive market, superprofits are unattainable. Businesses will do whatever is necessary to isolate themselves from the workings of the free market and competition, employing a variety of strategies and tools to sabotage and control the market. In the business of finance, these strategies work through sabotage of clients, competitors and the state.

The paradox of sabotage is that while it is ostensibly a behavioural problem, in finance it is both systemic and systematic. Within that sector the constant fight against competition and for market control means that our financial intermediaries – be they banks, new fintech start-ups or shadow banks – use their size, capital, innovation and command of technology to bypass existing regulations, grow in power and autonomy, undermine competitors and exploit customers and the public resource.

So What?

Sabotage in finance is also systematic, because it evolves dynamically through the regulatory cycle: augmenting existing markets, exploiting regulatory niches and carving out new ones, enabling financial businesses to avoid costs and socialize risks in times of crises.

So what? Shall we establish an Anti-Sabotage Commission, or a Ministry for Bad Behaviour? Perhaps not. But building on history, a Pecora-inspired approach to financial regulation in the twenty-first century can take several simple but important intellectual steps towards a more adequate regulatory framework:

1. Move beyond the binary dichotomy of 'market vs. regulation', and place the profitability quandary at the very core of any regulatory approach.
2. Make an important, even if politically unpopular, distinction between 'the market' and 'business', based on the acknowledgement that businesses want, first and foremost, to control the market, typically at the expense of the public.
3. Recognize that financial stability, on its own, does not mean that finance will serve the economy and society well. At best, stability simply reinforces the status quo; at worst, it breeds instability and feeds sabotage.
4. Build on the simple idea that the consumers of finance – you and me, old and new – need to be protected in this industry, because financial sabotage is both systemic and systematic. This protection is not a fine, barely legible footnote at the bottom of a contract for a new credit card, a loan or a security. Ideally, such protection should involve a set of institutional arrangements, with a proactive role for

the state, by which customers can really enjoy the benefits of competition in finance without having to compensate for the behaviour of the financiers.

5. Finally and perhaps most radically, we need to stop thinking about finance as a business of managing 'other people's money'. Finance is the business of creating and managing *our* wealth, and it needs to be understood and regulated as such.

ACKNOWLEDGEMENTS

In writing this book we relied on many friends and colleagues who work in finance or are clients of the industry. They patiently spent precious time with us, sharing their views and experiences of the financial sector. There are too many to list all of them, but we thank David Sassoon, Yoni Gluhovsky, Olessja Kantor, Karaca Mestci, Jean-Phillip Robe, Jessica Eistrand, and many others on both sides of the Atlantic who have spoken with us but prefer to be unnamed.

We are privileged to be surrounded by many bright people in our day jobs. Our colleagues at City, University of London, and elsewhere were the first readers of the chapters and generously provided feedback, despite the demands of their own workloads. We are very grateful to Amnon Aran, Albena Azmanova, Giselle Datz, Sandy Hager, Oliver Kessler, Iosif Kovras, Photis Lysandrou, Perry Mehrling, Stefano Pagliari, Inderjeet Parmar, Hannah Petersen, Richard Phillips, Brunello Rosa, Amin Samman, Stefano Sgambati, Atul Shah, Sara Silvestri, Mark (Herman) Schwartz, Jan Toporowski, and many others who have listened to our argument and helped make it more lucid. We are indebted to Anne

Acknowledgements

Henow and Anne Zimmerman, who assisted us with background research. Research on chapters 11 and 12 was supported by the Horizon 2020 COFFERS grant (EU grant agreement 727145).

This book would not have come to fruition without the interest, encouragement and support of one person: James Pullen of the Wylie Agency. His enthusiasm for the project, advice and, crucially, patience have guided us along the tricky path of translating academic theories and jargon into a text which would be accessible and interesting to the wider public. We have been lucky with our editors: Thomas Penn of Penguin and Clive Priddle of PublicAffairs. Their teams have been fantastically efficient and highly professional.

BIBLIOGRAPHY

Amadeo, K., 'Bearn Stearns, Its Collapse, and Bailout', The Balance, 8 October 2018 (updated), www.thebalance.com/bearn-stearns-collapse-and -bailout-3305613.

Arnold, M., 'Banks pay lowest proportion of tax since before financial crisis', *Financial Times*, 4 December 2015.

Arnold, M., 'RBS settles DoJ fraud claims over mortgage-backed securities', *Financial Times*, 26 October 2017, www.ft.com/content/2231f092 -f991-3eef-9ebe-4a46ed6ddf9f.

Arnold, M., et. al., 'Banking M&A: the quest to create a European champion', *Financial Times*, 11 July 2018, www.ft.com/content/cd640614-78a1 -11e8-8e67-1e1a0846c475.

Arrow, K. J., 'Rational Choice Functions and Orderings', *Economia*, vol. 26, 1959, pp. 121–7, https://doi.org/10.2307/2550390.

Aubry, Manon, and Thomas Dauphin, 'Opening the Vaults: The Use of Tax Havens by Europe's Biggest Banks', Oxfam, 2017.

Augar, P., *The Death of Gentlemanly Capitalism: The Rise and Fall of London's Investment Banks*, Penguin Books, 2008.

Austin, H., 'Five of world's biggest investment banks pay no UK corporation tax', *Independent*, 23 December 2015, www.independent.co.uk /news/business/news/five-of-worlds-biggest-investment-banks-pay -no-uk-corporation-tax-a6783716.html.

Bibliography

Awrey, D., 'Toward a Supply-Side Theory of Financial Innovation', *Journal of Comparative Economics*, vol. 41:2, 2013, p. 401.

Bain, J., 'The Profit Rate as a Measure of Monopoly Power', *Quarterly Journal of Economics*, vol. 55:2, 1 February 1941, pp. 271–93, https://doi.org/10.2307/1882062.

Bank Confidential, Letter to Treasury Select Committee, House of Commons, London, 28 January 2018, TSC/BC/WB/10118, https://bankconfidential.com/wp-content/uploads/2018/02/TSC-Final-letter-1-1.pdf.

Bateman, O., 'Bitcoin might make tax havens obsolete', Motherboard, *Vice*, 22 June 2016, https://motherboard.vice.com/en_us/article/wnxzpy/bitcoin-might-make-tax-havens-obsolete.

Benston, G. J., W. C. Hunter and L. D. Wall, 'Motivations for Bank Mergers and Acquisitions: Enhancing the Deposit Insurance Put Option versus Earnings Diversification', *Journal of Money, Credit and Banking*, vol. 27, 1995, pp. 777–88, https://doi.org/10.2307/2077749.

Berstein, P., *Against the Gods: The Remarkable Story of Risk*, John Wiley and Sons, 1998.

Binham, C., 'RBS unit memo told staff to let clients "hang themselves"', *Financial Times*, 17 January 2018.

Binham, C., 'MPs slam "regulatory black hole" for bank lending to small business', *Financial Times*, 26 October 2018, www.ft.com/content/551fb48a-d875-11e8-a854-33d6f82e62f8.

Bloomberg, 'Emilio Botin', 17 June 2002, https://web.archive.org/web/20110601110648; www.businessweek.com:80/magazine/content/02_24/b3787634.htm.

Bowers, S., 'London business figures embroiled in Kaupthing fraud investigation', *Guardian*, 6 June 2010, www.theguardian.com/business/2010/jun/06/kaupthing-deutsch-bank-iceland.

Boyce, L., 'I worked at RBS during the financial crisis – and sales pressure is now ten times worse': dozens more whistleblowers step forward to tell of bank misery', This is Money, 4 August 2016, www.thisismoney.co.uk/money/saving/article-3712765/Dozens-RBS-staff-tell-hard-sales-pressure-branches.html.

Boyd, R., 'The last days of Bear Stearns', *Fortune*, 31 March 2008, http://archive.fortune.com/2008/03/28/magazines/fortune/boyd_bear.fortune/index.htm.

Bibliography

Braithwaite, T., 'Dimon warns breaking up JPMorgan would hurt US financial power', *Financial Times*, 14 January 2015, www.ft.com/content /7e907a18-9c04-11e4-a6b6-00144feabdc0.

Brandeis, L. D., *Other People's Money: And How the Bankers Use It*, F. A. Stokes, 1914.

Braudel, F., *Civilization and Capitalism, 15th–18th Century*, vol. 3: *Perspective of the World*, University of California Press, Berkeley, 1992.

Braudel, F., *Civilization & Capitalism 15th–18th Century*, vol. 2: *The Wheels of Commerce*, new edn, Weidenfeld and Nicolson, 2002.

Bray, C., 'Goldman Sachs didn't trick Libyan fund', *The New York Times*, 14 October 2016, www.nytimes.com/2016/10/15/business/dealbook/goldman-sachs-libya-sovereign-wealth-fund.html.

Brewer, E., and J. Jagtiani, 'How Much Did Banks Pay to Become Too-Big-To-Fail and to Become Systemically Important?' *Journal of Financial Services Research*, vol. 43, 2013, pp. 1–35, https://doi.org/10.1007/s10693 -011-0119-6.

Bristow, T., 'Four hotels, an £8m firm, all gone – one Norfolk hotelier's battle with RBS', *Eastern Daily Press*, 21 March 2018, www.edp24.co.uk /business/hotelier-david-easter-rbs-grg-turnaround-norfolk-1-5443669.

Burgis, T., 'Dark money: London's dirty secret', *Financial Times*, 11 May 2016, www.ft.com/content/1d805534-1185-11e6-839f-2922947098f0.

Burrough, B., 'Bringing Down Bear Stearns', *Vanity Fair*, 30 June 2008, www.vanityfair.com/news/2008/08/bear_stearns200808-2.

Carney, M., 'The Promise of FinTech – Something New under the Sun?', speech at the Bank of England, 25 January 2017, www.bankofengland .co.uk/speech/2017/the-promise-of-fintech-something-new-under-the -sun.

Clifford Chance LLP, 'Independent Review of the Central Allegation Made by Dr Lawrence Tomlinson in Banks' Lending Practices: Treatment of Businesses in Distress', 2011, www.rbs.com/content/dam/rbs_com/rbs /Documents/News/2014/04/Clifford-Chance-Independent-Review.pdf.

Chaunu, P., *La Civilisation de l'Europe des lumières: 239 héliogravures...*, Flammarion, 1971.

Chincarini, L., *The Crisis of Crowding: Quant Copycats, Ugly Models, and the New Crash Normal*, John Wiley and Sons, 2012.

Bibliography

Clark, A., 'Former Bear Stearns boss Jimmy Cayne blames conspiracy for bank's collapse', *Guardian*, 5 May 2010, www.theguardian.com/busi ness/2010/may/05/bear-stearns-boss-denies-blame [accessed 23 June 2017.

CNN, 'ICO Scams Have Raised More Than $1 Billion, Report Claims', 19 May 2018, www.ccn.com/ico-scams-have-raised-more-than-1-billion-report -claims.

Cohan, W., 'Michael Milken invented the modern junk bond, went to prison, and then became one of the most respected people on Wall Street', *Business Insider*, 2 May 2017, http://uk.businessinsider.com/michael-mil ken-life-story-2017-5?r=US&IR=T.

Cohan, William D., *House of Cards: How Wall Street's Gamblers Broke Capitalism*, Allen Lane, 2009, pp. 244–53.

Commons, J. R., *Institutional Economics*, vol. 1: *Its Place in Political Economy*, Transaction Publishers, 1990.

Commons, J. R., *Legal Foundations of Capitalism*, reprint edn, Lawbook Exchange, 2012

Corey, L., *The House of Morgan: A Social Biography of the Masters of Money*, G. H. Watt, 1930.

Crotty, J., 'If Financial Market Competition Is So Intense, Why Are Financial Firm Profits So High? Reflections on the Current "Golden Age" of Finance', University of Massachusetts, Amherst, PERI Working Paper Series, No. 134, April 2007.

Cuomo, A., 'No Rhyme or Reason. The Heads I Win, Tails You Lose Bank Bonus Culture', workplacebullying.org/multi/pdf/Cuomo.pdf, 2009.

Darrah, K., 'The QE reversal', *World Finance*, 26 April 2018, www.world finance.com/banking/the-qe-reversal.

Davíðsdóttir, S., 'What is Deutsche Bank hiding in Iceland?', Sigrún Davíðsdóttir's Icelog, undated, http://uti.is/?s=deutsche.

Davidson, A., 'How AIG fell apart', Reuters, 18 September 2008, www .reuters.com/article/us-how-aig-fell-apart-idUSMAR85972720080918.

Deutsche Bank, Annual Report, 2016, www.db.com/ir/en/download /Deutsche_Bank_Annual_Report_2016.pdf.

Donohoe, P., 'How often is the 'Single Malt' tax loophole used? The government is finding out', The Journal, 15 November 2017, www.thejournal .ie/single-malt-tax-evasion-3698512-Nov2017.

Bibliography

Economist, 'Credit Derivatives: The Great Untangling', 6 November 2008, www.economist.com/briefing/2008/11/06/the-great-untangling.

Economist, 'Scots on the Rocks', 25 February 2010, www.economist .com/briefing/2010/02/25/scots-on-the-rocks.

Economist, 'The Stars of the Junkyard', 21 October 2010.

Edmonds, T., ' Treatment of SMEs by RBS Global Restructuring Group', Debate Pack, House of Commons Library, 16 January 2018, researchbrief ings.files.parliament.uk/documents/CDP-2018…/CDP-2018-0011.pdf.

Egan, M., '5,300 Wells Fargo employees fired over 2 million phony accounts', CNN Business, 8 September 2016, money.cnn.com/2016/09/08 /investing/wells-fargo-created-phony-accounts-bank-fees/index.html.

Endlich, L., *Goldman Sachs: The Culture of Success*, Touchstone, 2000.

Erman, M., and H. Somerville, 'LendingClub says ex-CEO took loans to boost volumes', Reuters, 28 June 2016, www.reuters.com/article/us -lendingclub-ceo-idUSKCN0ZE13Q.

Fama, E., 'Efficient Capital Markets: A Review of Theory and Empirical Work', *Journal of Finance*, vol. 25:2, 1970.

Fame, W., and L. White, 'Empirical Studies of Financial Innovation: Lots of Talk, Little Action?', Working Paper 2002–12, Federal Reserve Bank of Atlanta, 2002.

FCIC (US Financial Crisis Inquiry Commission), 'The Financial Crisis Inquiry Report', Final Report of the National Commission on the Causes of the Financial and Economic Crisis in the United States, US Government Printing Office, January 2011, www.gpo.gov/fdsys/pkg/GPO-FCIC/pdf /GPO-FCIC.pdf.

Finextra, 'Fed researchers compare P2P lending to subprime mortgages', 10 November 2017, www.finextra.com/newsarticle/31322/fed-res earchers-compare-p2p-lending-to-subprime-mortgages.

Fino, Jessica, 'UK banks make £9bn in profits in tax havens', *Economia*, 27 March 2017, https://economia.icaew.com/news/march-2017/uk-banks -hold-9bn-in-profits-in-tax-havens.

Fiordelisi, F., 'Why Do Banks Merge?', in *Mergers and Acquisitions in European Banking*, Palgrave Macmillan Studies in Banking and Financial Institutions, Palgrave Macmillan, 2009, pp. 48–84 https://doi .org/10.1057/9780230245402_3.

Bibliography

Focarelli, D., F. Panetta and C. Salleo, 'Why Do Banks Merge?', *Journal of Money, Credit and Banking*, vol. 34, 2002, pp. 1047–66.

Fortune, 'America's Most Admired Companies', 2007, http://archive .fortune.com/magazines/fortune/mostadmired/2007/industries/indus try_52.html.

Fraser, I., 'Do Merrill Lynch bankers know no shame?', Ian Fraser blog, 23 January 2009, www.ianfraser.org/742.

Fraser, I., 'RBS executives seem to think they're above the law', Ian Fraser blog, 16 December 2010, www.ianfraser.org/rbs-executives-think -theyre-above-the-law.

Fraser, I., 'A short history of RBS's Global Restructuring Group', I am Fraser blog, 17 June 2012, www.ianfraser.org/has-rbs-become-a-rogue-insti tution.

Fraser, I., *Shredded: Inside RBS, the Bank That Broke Britain*, Birlinn, 2014.

Fraser, I., 'My nightmare 10-year battle for RBS damages: businessman in landmark court victory backs campaign for safeguards', *Financial Mail on Sunday*, 28 October 2017, www.thisismoney.co.uk/money/news/article -5027439/My-nightmare-10-year-battle-RBS-damages.html.

FTC (Federal Trade Commission], 'FTC charges Lending Club with deceiving consumers', press release, 25 April 2018, www.ftc.gov/news -events/press-releases/2018/04/ftc-charges-lending-club-deceiving -consumers-0.

Giannone, J., 'AIG bailout good for banks while investors bleed', Reuters, 11 March 2009, www.reuters.com/article/us-aig-bailout-sb-idUSTRE52A0 TP20090311.

Glazer, E., 'Whistleblowers detail Wells Fargo wealth management woes', *Wall Street Journal*, 27 July 2018, www.wsj.com/articles/whistle blowers-detail-wells-fargo-wealth-management-woes-1532707096.

Goldfarb, Z., 'Former Bear Stearns executives blame collapse on "self-fulfilling prophecy"', *Washington Post*, 6 May 2010, www.washingtonpost .com/wp-dyn/content/article/2010/05/05/AR2010050505104.html.

Goldman Sachs, Consent of Defendant Goldman, Sachs & Co., *SEC v. Goldman Sachs & Co.*, 790 F. Supp. 2d 147 (S.D.N.Y. 2011) (No. 10-CV-3229), 2010 WL 2779309, 2010.

Bibliography

Graeber, D., *Debt: The First Five Thousand Years*, Melville House Publishing, 2013.

Griffin, R., et al., 'How Azerbaijan's biggest bank used Dublin on way to default', *Irish Times*, 19 June 2017, www.irishtimes.com/business/fin ancial-services/how-azerbaijan-s-biggest-bank-used-dublin-on-way -to-default-1.3124981.

Haldane, A., 'On being the Right Size', speech at the Institute of Economic Affairs, 22nd Annual Series, The 2012 Beesley Lectures, at the Institute of Directors, London, 25 October 2012, www.bis.org/review/r121030d.pdf.

Haldane, A., 'The Age of Asset Management', speech at London Business School, 4 April 2014, www.bankofengland.co.uk/speech/2014/the -age-of-asset-management.

Handelsblatt, 'Beide Asien-Finanzchefs beurlaubt', 19 May 2015 (in German only), www.handelsblatt.com/unternehmen/management/deutsche -bank-beide-asien-finanzchefs-beurlaubt/11796824.html.

Hansard, Treasury Committee: Oral Evidence: 'RBS' Global Restructuring Group and its treatment of SMEs', HC 737, 30 January 2018, http://data .parliament.uk/writtenevidence/committeeevidence.svc/evidence document/treasury-committee/rbs-global-restructuring-group-and-its-treat ment-of-smes/oral/77683.html.

Harrison, W., 'In defence of big banks', *The New York Times*, 22 August 2012, www.nytimes.com/2012/08/23/opinion/dont-break-up-the-big-banks .html.

Hodgson, G. M., 'John R. Commons and the Foundations of Institutional Economics', *Journal of Economic Issues*, vol. 37, 2003, pp. 547–76, https://doi.org/10.1080/00213624.2003.11506603.

Hodgson, G. M., *The Evolution of Institutional Economics*, Routledge, 2004.

Hosters, J., 'Joseph Schumpeter and His Legacy in Innovation Studies', *Knowledge, Technology, & Policy*, vol. 18:3, 2005, pp. 20–37.

Independent, 'The banker the credit crisis couldn't touch', 27 July 2008, www.independent.co.uk/news/business/analysis-and-features/the -banker-the-credit-crisis-couldnt-touch-878002.html.

Ingram, D. and P. Rudegeair, 'U.S. accuses Bank of America of mortgage-backed securities fraud', Reuters, 6 August 2013, https://uk.reuters.com /article/us-bofa-justice-idUSBRE9750ZU20130806.

Bibliography

Jenkins, P. and L. Noonan, 'How Deutsche Bank's high-stakes gamble went wrong', *Financial Times*, 9 November 2017, www.ft.com/content/60 fa7da6-c414-11e7-a1d2-6786f39ef675.

Josephson, M., *The Robber Barons: The Great American Capitalists 1861–1901*, Harcourt Brace, 1962.

Kaminska, I., 'Fintech's security/access paradox problem', *Financial Times*, 3 October 2016, https://ftalphaville.ft.com/2016/10/03/2176471/fin techs-securityaccess-paradox-problem.

Kaminska, I., 'Fintech as a gateway for criminal enterprise', *Financial Times*, 'Alphaville', 12 January 2018, https://ftalphaville.ft.com/2018/01/12 /2197610/fintech-as-a-gateway-for-criminal-enterprise.

Katz, L., 'Criminals may ditch Bitcoin for Litecoin, Dash, study says', Bloomberg, 8 February 2018, https://www.bloomberg.com/news/articles /2018-02-08/criminals-are-ditching-bitcoin-for-litecoin-and-dash -study-says.

Kay, J., *Other People's Money: Masters of the Universe or Servants of the People?*, Profile Books, 2015.

Kelly, K., 'EC will scour Bear trading data', *Wall Street Journal*, 28 May 2008, www.wsj.com/articles/SB121193543321324769.

Kelly, K, *Street Fighters: The Last 72 Hours of Bear Stearns, the Toughest Firm on Wall Street*, Penguin Books, 2009.

Kelly, K. and S. Craig, 'Goldman is queried about Bear's fall', *Wall Street Journal*, 16 July 2008, www.wsj.com/articles/SB121617167587756521.

Kelso, E., 'New study: 80% of ICOs are scams, only 8% reach an exchange', Bitcoin.com, 28 March 2018, https://news.bitcoin.com/80-of-icos -are-scams-only-8-reach-an-exchange.

Ketchum, D., '15 biggest crowdfunding scams and failures of all time', Go Banking Rates, 14 March 2018, www.gobankingrates.com/making-money /business/biggest-crowdfunding-scams-failures.

Kottasowa, I., '9 trillion and counting: how central banks are still flooding the world with money', CNN Business, 9 September 2016, https:// money.cnn.com/2016/09/08/news/economy/central-banks-printed-nine -trillion/index.html.

Kummer, S. and C. Pauletto, 'The History of Derivatives: A Few Mile-

Bibliography

stones', EFTA Seminar on Regulation of Derivatives Markets, Zurich, 3 May 2012, SECO and Federal Department of Economic Affairs FDEA, www.seco .admin.ch/…/History_of_Derivatives…/10%20The%20History%20of…

Larsen, P., 'Lever again', Reuters, 27 December 2017, www.breakingviews .com/features/regulators-will-drive-next-wave-of-eu-bank-mergers.

Lavoie, M., 2009, *Introduction to Post-Keynesian Economics*, Palgrave Macmillan.

Levine, M., 'Abacus CDO bites Goldman back', Bloomberg, 26 September 2018, www.bloomberg.com/opinion/articles/2018-09-26/abacus-cdo -bites-goldman-back.

Levine, M., 'Wells Fargo opened a couple million fake accounts', Bloomberg, 9 September 2016, www.bloomberg.com/opinion/articles/2016 -09-09/wells-fargo-opened-a-couple-million-fake-accounts.

Lopez, L., 'The IRS is getting serious about cracking down on another cherished hedge fund tax loophole', Business Insider, 1 July 2013, www .businessinsider.com/irs-eyes-basket-options-tax-loophole-2013-7?IR=T.

Makowski, L., and J. M. Ostroy, 'Perfect Competition and the Creativity of the Market', *Journal of Economic Literature*, vol. 39, 2001, pp. 479–535, https://doi.org/10.1257/jel.39.2.479.

Manager Magazin, 'Deutsche bank zahlt 450 Millionen im Kaupthing Vergleich', 22 March 2017, www.manager-magazin.de/unternehmen/ban ken/deutsche-bank-offenbar-450-millionen-im-kaupthing-vergleich -gezahlt-a-1139859.html.

Mason, R., 'Bankrupt Cayman Islands to get £38m bail-out', *Telegraph*, 30 September 2009, www.telegraph.co.uk/finance/financialcrisis/6248284 /Bankrupt-Cayman-Islands-to-get-38m-bail-out.html.

McKinnon, R., *Money and Capital in Economic Development*, Brookings Institution, 1973.

McLean, B., and J. Nocera, *All the Devils Are Here: Unmasking the Men Who Blew Up the World*, Viking, 2010.

Megaw, N., 'RBS ranked UK's least popular bank', *Financial Times*, 15 August 2018, www.ft.com/content/60c95b72-a05a-11e8-85da-eeb7a9ce36e4.

Mehrling, P., *The New Lombard Street*, Princeton University Press, 2010.

Minsky, H., *Stabilizing an Unstable Economy*, Yale University Press, 1986.

Bibliography

Monaghan, A., 'Too big to fail' risks growing in asset management', *Guardian*, 4 April 2014, www.theguardian.com/business/2014/apr/04/as set-management-risks-bailout-rising-warns-bank-of-england.

Moody's, 'Danièle Nouy of ECB on consolidation in European banking sector', 27 September 2017, www.moodysanalytics.com/regulatory-news /sept-27-daniele-nouy-of-ecb-on-consolidation-in-european-banking-sector.

Morgan, D. P., and K. J. Stiroh, *Too Big to Fail after All These Years* (SSRN Scholarly Paper No. ID 813967), Social Science Research Network, 2005.

Morgentson, G., 'A Bank Too Big to Jail', *The New York Times*, 15 July 2016, www.nytimes.com/2016/07/17/business/a-bank-too-big-to-jail.html.

Moscow Times, 'Deutsche Bank Moscow faces three investigations over possible money laundering', 16 July 2015, https://themoscowtimes.com /articles/deutsche-bank-moscow-faces-three-investigations-over-possible -money-laundering-48219.

Nasiripour, S., 'Largest banks likely profited by borrowing from Federal Reserve, lending to Federal Government', Huffington Post, 26 April 2011, www.huffingtonpost.co.uk/entry/fed-lending-helped-wall-street_n _853884.

Newman, D., 'Exploring 5 trends driving the fintech revolution', *Forbes*, 3 July 2018, www.forbes.com/sites/danielnewman/2018/07/03/exploring -5-trends-driving-the-fintech-revolution/#3a83941812c7.

Noonan, L., and P. Jenkins, 'JPMorgan: defying attempts to end "too big to fail"', *Financial Times*, 12 September 2018, www.ft.com/content/0e ebc7de-b4de-11e8-b3ef-799c8613f4a1.

Norris, F., 'Naked truth on default swaps', *The New York Times*, 10 May 2010, www.nytimes.com/2010/05/21/business/economy/21norris.html?mt rref=www.google.com.

O' Hara, M., and W. Shaw, 'Deposit Insurance and Wealth Effects: The Value of Being 'Too Big to Fail', *Journal of Finance*, vol. 45, 1990, pp. 1587– 1600, https://doi.org/10.1111/j.1540-6261.1990.tb03729.x.

Partnoy, F., *FIASCO: Blood in the Water on Wall Street*, Profile Books, 2009.

Partz, H., 'SEC launches mock ICO to show investors warning signs of fraud', Coin Telegraph, 16 May 2018, https://cointelegraph.com/news/sec -launches-mock-ico-to-show-investors-warning-signs-of-fraud.

Peston, R., 'How hedge funds sunk Bear Stearns', BBC News, 14 March

Bibliography

2008, www.bbc.co.uk/blogs/thereporters/robertpeston/2008/03/how_hedge
_funds_sunk_bear_stea.html.

Pickard, J., and S. Goff, 'Santander can bid for RBS business branches', *Financial Times*, 1 November 2009, www.ft.com/content/51c343e4-c72a -11de-bb6f-00144feab49a.

Piketty, T., *Capital in the 21st Century*, Harvard University Press, 2014.

Piskorski, T., A. Seru and J. Witkin, 'Asset Quality Misrepresentation by Financial Intermediaries: Evidence from RMBS Market', Kreisman Working Paper Series in Housing Law and Policy, No. 9, University of Chicago Law School, 2013, https://chicagounbound.uchicago.edu/cgi/viewcontent.cgi ?article=1006&context=housing_law_and_policy.

Polillo, S., *Conservatives vs Wildcats: A Sociology of Financial Conflict*, Stanford University Press, 2013.

Press Association, 'Barclays agrees to pay $2bn to settle US fraud case', *Guardian*, 29 March 2018 www.theguardian.com/business/2018/mar /29/barclays-agrees-to-pay-2bn-to-settle-us-case-justice-department -mortgage-backed-securities.

Price, M., and P. Schroeder, 'Trump's consumer financial chief disbands key advisory boards', Reuters, 6 June 2018, www.reuters.com/article /us-usa-cfpb-boards/trumps-consumer-financial-chief-disbands-key -advisory-boards-idUSKCN1J22PN.

Promontory Financial Group, 'RBS Group Treatment of the SME Customers Referred to the Global Restructuring Group', report prepared for the FCA, September 2016, www.parliament.uk/documents/commons-com mittees/treasury/s166-rbs-grg.pdf.

Puri, M., 'Commercial Banks in Investment Banking Conflict of Interest or Certification Role?', *Journal of Financial Economics*, vol. 40:3, 1996, https://doi.org/10.1016/0304-405X(95)00855-9.

Ranawake, N., 'There is no debate; the country needs bigger and stronger banks', Daily FT, 29 June 2018, www.ft.lk/financial-services/%E2 %80%9C-There-is-no-debate-the-country-needs-bigger-and-stronger -banks-%E2%80%9D/42-657994.

Reuters, 'Banks paid $321 billion in fines since financial crisis: BCG', 2 March 2017, www.reuters.com/article/us-banks-fines/banks-paid-321 -billion-in-fines-since-financial-crisis-bcg-idUSKBN1692Y2.

Bibliography

Riesman, D., *Thorstein Veblen*, Transaction Publishers, 1953.

Robinson, E., and M. Montijano, 'Santander's Ana Botin has something to prove', Bloomberg, 23 November 2015, www.bloomberg.com/news/features/2015-11-23/santander-s-ana-bot-n-has-something-to-prove.

Robinson, G., 'Kaupthing: We're not – repeat NOT – desperate', *Financial Times*, 'Alphaville', 5 March 2008, https://ftalphaville.ft.com/2008/03/05/11367/kaupthing-were-not-repeat-not-desperate/?source=rss.

Roe, M. J., 'Structural Corporate Degradation Due to Too-Big-to-Fail Finance', *University of Pennsylvania Law Review*, vol. 162, 2014, pp. 1419–64.

Rosenbaum, E., 'Goldman Sachs stock: buy, sell or hold?', The Street, 20 April 2010, www.thestreet.com/story/10728591/1/goldman-sachs-stock-buy-sell-or-hold.html.

Rucker, P., 'Exclusive: Wells Fargo faces sanctions for auto insurance payouts – sources', Reuters, 15 March 2018, www.reuters.com/article/us-wells-fargo-accounts-auto-exclusive/exclusive-wells-fargo-faces-sanctions-for-auto-insurance-payouts-sources-idUSKCN1GR0G3.

Rudegeair, P., 'Lending Club CEO Fired over Faulty Loans', *Wall Street Journal*, 9 May 2016, www.wsj.com/articles/lendingclub-ceo-resigns-over-sales-review-1462795070.

Samuelson, P. A., 'Proof That Properly Anticipated Prices Fluctuate Randomly', in *The World Scientific Handbook of Futures Markets* (World Scientific Handbook in Financial Economics Series), *World Scientific*, 2015, pp. 25–38, https://doi.org/10.1142/9789814566926_0002.

Schäfer, D., et al., 'Barclays in Qatar loan probe', *Financial Times*, 30 January 2013, www.ft.com/content/47d412ce-6bd1-11e2-a700-00144feab49a.

Schumpeter, J. A., 'The Influence of Protective Tariffs on the Industrial Development of the United States', *Proceedings of the Academy of Political Science*, vol. 19:1, 1940, pp. 2–7.

Schwarz, H., *Subprime Nation: American Power, Global Capital and the Housing Bubble*, Cornell University Press, 2009.

Seager, A., L. Elliot and J. Kollewe, 'Barclays admits borrowing hundreds of millions at Bank's emergency rate', *Guardian*, 31 August 2007, www.theguardian.com/business/2007/aug/31/money.

SEC, Complaint, Litigation Release, 2010, www.sec.gov/litigation/complaints/2010/comp-pr2010-59.pdf.

Bibliography

Senate Committee on Banking and Currency, 'The Pecora Report: The 1934 Report on the Practices of Stock Exchanges from the Pecora Commission', US Senate, Report No. 1455, Washinghton, DC, June 2009 [1934], www.senate.gov/artandhistory/history/common/.../pdf/Pecora_Final Report.pdf.

Smith, G., *Why I Left Goldman Sachs: A Wall Street Story*, Grand Central Publishing, 2012.

Strange, S., *States and Markets*, Continuum, 1988.

Telegraph, 'RBS and Barclays should both be getting the jitters', 'Comment', 28 July 2007, www.telegraph.co.uk/finance/comment/2813039/RBS -and-Barclays-should-both-be-getting-the-jitters.html.

Tett, G., *Fool's Gold: How Unrestrained Greed Corrupted a Dream, Shattered Global Markets and Unleashed a Catastrophe*, Abacus, 2009.

Thornton, J., 'The Financial Repression Paradigm: A Survey of Empirical Research', *Savings and Development*, vol. 15:1, 1991, pp. 5–18.

Treanor, J., 'RBS facing £400m bill to compensate small business customers', *Guardian*, 8 November 2016, www.theguardian.com/business/2016 /nov/08/rbs-facing-400m-bill-to-compensate-small-business-customers.

Tully, S., 'Lewie Ranieri wants to fix the mortgage mess', *Fortune*, 9 December 2009, http://archive.fortune.com/2009/12/08/real_estate/lewie _ranieri_mortgages.fortune/index.htm.

US Senate, 'Abuse of Structured Products', Majority and Minority Staff Report, Permanent Subcommittee on Investigations, 22 July 2014 hearing, www.gpo.gov/fdsys/pkg/CHRG-113shrg89882/pdf/CHRG-113shrg89 882.pdf.

Veblen, T., *Why Is Economics Not an Evolutionary Science?*, Quarterly Journal of Economics, vol. 12, 1898, pp. 373–97, https://doi.org/10.2307/1882952.

Veblen, T., *The Vested Interests and the Common Man*, abridged edn, Cosimo Classics, New York, 2005.

Veblen, T., *Absentee Ownership: Business Enterprise in Recent Times – The Case of America*, Routledge, 2017, https://doi.org/10.4324/9781315083148.

Veblen, T., *The Engineers & the Price System: From the Author of The Theory of the Leisure Class, The Theory of Business Enterprise, Imperial Germany and the Industrial Revolution & The Higher Learning in America*, Musaicum Books, 2017.

Bibliography

Veblen, T., *The Theory of the Leisure Class*, Routledge, 2017, https://doi.org/10.4324/9781315135373.

Wallace, T., 'Goldman Sachs accused of "taking advantage" of naive Libyans who "live in the middle of the desert with camels"', *Telegraph*, 13 June 2016, www.telegraph.co.uk/business/2016/06/13/goldman-sachs-accused-of-taking-advantage-of-naive-libyans-who-l.

Weber, E., 'A Short History of Derivative Security Markets', SSRN Working Paper, June 2008, https://papers.ssrn.com/sol3/papers.cfm?abstract_id=1141689.

Werdingier, J., 'Barclays withdraws bid to take over ABN-Amro', *The New York Times*, 6 October 2007, www.nytimes.com/2007/10/06/business/worldbusiness/06bank.html.

Wheelock, D., 'Too Big to Fail: The Pros and Cons of Breaking Up Big Banks', Regional Economist, St Louis Fed, October 2012, www.stlouisfed.org/publications/regional-economist/october-2012/too-big-to-fail-the-pros-and-cons-of-breaking-up-big-banks.

Wieczner, J., 'Bitcoin investors aren't paying their cryptocurrency taxes', *Fortune*, 13 February 2018, http://fortune.com/2018/02/13/bitcoin-cryptocurrency-tax-taxes.

Wildau, G., and Y. Jia, 'Collapse of Chinese peer-to-peer lenders sparks investor flight', *Financial Times*, 22 July 2018, www.ft.com/content/75e75628-8b27-11e8-bf9e-8771d5404543.

Wilson, H., P. Aldrick and K. Ahmed, 'RBS investigation: Chapter 2 – the ABN Amro takeover', *Telegraph*, 11 December 2011, www.telegraph.co.uk/finance/newsbysector/banksandfinance/8947530/RBS-investigation-Chapter-2-the-ABN-Amro-takeover.html.

Wolf, M., 'Banking remains far too undercapitalised for comfort', *Financial Times*, 21 September 2017, www.ft.com/content/9dd43a1a-9d49-11e7-8cd4-932067fbf946.

REFERENCES AND NOTES

Introduction: Everyone Wants to Be like Goldman

1. T. Wallace, 'Goldman Sachs accused of "taking advantage" of naive Libyans who "live in the middle of the desert with camels"', *Telegraph*, 13 June 2016.

2. C. Bray, 'Goldman Sachs didn't trick Libyan fund', *The New York Times*, 14 October 2016.

3. L. Endlich, *Goldman Sachs: The Culture of Success*, Touchstone, 2000.

4. SEC, www.sec.gov/news/press/2010/2010-59.htm, 2010.

5. Litigation Release No. 21489, 16 April 2010.

6. G. Smith, *Why I Left Goldman Sachs: A Wall Street Story*, Grand Central Publishing, 2012.

7. P. A. Samuelson, 'Proof That Properly Anticipated Prices Fluctuate Randomly', in *The World Scientific Handbook of Futures Markets* (World Scientific Handbook in Financial Economics Series), World Scientific, 2015, ch. 2, pp. 25–38.

8. T. Burgis, 'Dark money: London's dirty secret', *Financial Times*, 11 May 2016, www.ft.com/content/1d805534-1185-11e6-839f-2922947098f0.

9. 'Deutsche Bank Moscow faces three investigations over possible money laundering', *Moscow Times*, 16 July 2015; https://themoscowtimes.com/articles/deutsche-bank-moscow-faces-three-investigations-over-possible-money-laundering-48219.

Notes on Introduction

10. www.finance-watch.org/hot-topics/blog/1186-jenkins-bank-misdeeds.

11. T. Veblen, *The Engineers & the Price System: From the Author of The Theory of the Leisure Class, The Theory of Business Enterprise, Imperial Germany and the Industrial Revolution & The Higher Learning in America*, Musaicum Books, 2017.

12. Senate Committee on Banking and Currency, 1934, pp. 3–4.

PART ONE. SABOTAGE AS AN ECONOMIC CONCEPT

Chapter 1. Sabotage in the Financial System

1. The school is known as evolutionary economics or old institutional economics. It is associated primarily with the works of Thorstein Veblen and John R. Commons. For broad discussion of the old school of evolutionary economics see: J. Hodgson, *The Evolution of Institutional Economics*, Routledge, 2004, and J. Hodgson, 'John R. Commons and the Foundations of Institutional Economics', *Journal of Economic Issues*, 37, 2003, pp. 547–76.

2. T. Veblen, *The Engineers & the Price System: From the Author of The Theory of the Leisure Class, The Theory of Business Enterprise, Imperial Germany and the Industrial Revolution & The Higher Learning in America*, Musaicum Books, 2017, p. 4.

3. Ibid., p. 5.

4. J. Crotty, 'If Financial Market Competition Is So Intense, Why Are Financial Firm Profits So High?: Reflections on the Current "Golden Age" of Finance', University of Massachusetts Amherst, PERI Working Paper Series, No. 134, April 2007, p. 2.

5. J. Bain, 'The Profit Rate as a Measure of Monopoly Power', *The Quarterly Journal of Economics*, vol. 55, no. 2, 1 February 1941, pp. 271–93, https://doi.org/10.2307/1882062.

6. K. J. Arrow, 'Rational Choice Functions and Orderings', *Economica*, vol. 26, 1959, pp. 121–7, https://doi.org/10.2307/2550390.

7. 'Excess profits', Bain says, 'whatever the figure for such excesses might be, are a sure sign that the market is in some sort of dis-equilibria.' Alternatively, disequilibria are due to monopoly: 'although excess profits

218

Notes on Chapter 1

are thus not a sure indication of monopoly, they are, *if persisted*, a probable indication' (Bain, ' Profit Rate as a Measure of Monopoly Power').

8. In other words, the state, a political entity that Hayekians tend to scorn.

9. K. Ward, *Marketing Finance: Turning Marketing Strategies into Shareholder Value*, 3rd edn, Routledge, 2011, p. 1.

10. Makowski and Ostroy, 'Perfect Competition and the Creativity of the Market', *Journal of Economic Literature*, vol. 39, 2001, pp. 479–535, https://doi.org/10.1257/jel.39.2.479.

11. L. Corey, *The House of Morgan: A Social Biography of the Masters of Money*, G. H. Watt, 1930, p. 193.

12. Ibid., p. 245.

13. T. Veblen, *Absentee Ownership: Business Enterprise in Recent Times – The Case of America*, Transaction Publishers, 2017, pp. 40–41.

14. Ibid., p. 42.

15. Ibid., p. 47.

16. L. D. Brandeis, *Other People's Money: And How the Bankers Use It*, F. A. Stokes, 1914, p. 4.

17. In 2015, John Kay revisited the concept of OPM from the perspective of the twenty-first century (J. Kay, *Other People's Money: Masters of the Universe or Servants of the People?*, Profile Books, 2015).

18. Corey, *House of Morgan*.

19. Ibid., p. 448.

20. Ibid., p. 404.

21. Senate Committee on Banking and Currency, 'The Pecora Report: The 1934 Report on the Practices of Stock Exchanges from the Pecora Commission', US Senate, Report No. 1455, Washington, DC: June 2009 [1934], www.senate.gov/artandhistory/history/common/.../pdf/Pecora_Final Report.pdf.

22. M. Josephson, *The Robber Barons: The Great American Capitalists, 1861 to 1901*, Eyre and Spottiswoode, 1962, p. 411.

23. Senate Committee on Banking and Currency, 'Pecora Report', p. 396.

24. Inflation combined with stagnation, for which they blamed Keynesian policies.

25. Some of the bestsellers include: F. Partnoy, *Fiasco: Blood in the Water on Wall Street*, Profile Books, 2009; M. Lewis, *Liar's Poker: Two Cities, True Greed*, Hodder and Stoughton, 1989; S. Das, *Traders, Guns and Money: Knowns and Unknowns of the Dazzling World of Derivatives*, Prentice Hall, 2006.

26. M. Puri, 'Commercial Banks in Investment Banking: Conflict of Interest or Certification Role?', *Journal of Financial Economics*, vol. 40, 1996, pp. 373–401; G. J. Benston, W. C. Hunter and L. D. Wall, 'Motivations for Bank Mergers and Acquisitions: Enhancing the Deposit Insurance Put Option versus Earnings Diversification', *Journal of Money, Credit and Banking*, vol. 27, 1995, pp. 777–88.

27. J. Spindler, 'Conflict or Credibility: Research Analyst Conflicts of Interest and the Market for Underwriting Business', *Journal of Legal Studies*, vol. 35, no. 2, June 2006, pp. 303–25.

28. The recently introduced MIFID 2 directive prohibits free advice in the financial sector.

Chapter 2. Sabotage and the Cycle of Debt

1. www.imsdb.com/scripts/Margin-Call.html.

2. D. Graeber, *Debt: The First Five Thousand Years*, Melville House Publishing, 2013.

3. S. Strange, *States and Markets*, Continuum, 1988.

4. An exaggeration, no doubt, as finance is practically as old as humanity. Fama is not even the originator of the core ideas at the heart of contemporary financial economics known as the efficient market theory. The idea can be traced back to Paul Samuelson, whose contribution is neatly summarized by the title of his article 'Proof That Properly Anticipated Prices Fluctuate Randomly', in *The World Scientific Handbook of Futures Markets* ('World Scientific Handbook in Financial Economics Series', World Scientific, 2015, ch. 2, pp. 25–38. In an informationally efficient market, price changes must be unforecastable if they are properly anticipated, that is, if they fully incorporate the expectations and information of all market participants.

5. E. Fama, 'Efficient Capital Markets: A Review of Theory and Empirical Work', *Journal of Finance*, vol. 25:2, 1970, p. 383. According to Fama, in

Notes on Chapter 2

a fully efficient market, firms can make production-investment decisions, and investors can choose among the securities that represent ownership of firms' activities under the assumption that security prices at any time 'fully reflect' all available information.

6. The concept belongs to Perry Mehrling (*The New Lombard Street*, Princeton University Press, 2010).

7. P. Berstein, *Against the Gods: The Remarkable Story of Risk*, John Wiley and Sons, 1998.

8. E. Weber, 'A Short History of Derivative Security Markets', SSRN Working Paper, June 2008, https://papers.ssrn.com/sol3/papers.cfm?abstract_id=1141689.

9. S. Kummer and C. Pauletto, 'The History of Derivatives: A Few Milestones', EFTA Seminar on Regulation of Derivatives Markets, Zurich, 3 May 2012, State Secretariat for Economic Affairs and Federal Department of Economic Affairs.

10. Kummer and Pauletto, 'History of Derivatives'.

11. J. Huizinga, *Homo Ludens: A Study of the Play-Element in Culture*, Beacon Press, 1971, p. 16. See https://archive.org/details/in.ernet.dli.2015.100122/page/n19.

12. F. Braudel, *Civilization & Capitalism, 15th–18th Century*, vol. 2: *The Wheels of Commerce*, Weidenfeld and Nicolson, 2002, and vol. 3: *The Perspective of the World*, University of California Press, Berkeley, 1992; P. Chaunu, *La Civilisation de l'Europe des Lumières: 239 Héliogravures…*, Flammarion, 1971.

13. Mainly through the creation of institutions such as the Federal Mortgage Insurance Association (Fannie Mae) and Federal Home Loan Mortgage Corporation (Freddie Mac) in the US.

14. H. Schwarz, *Subprime Nation: America Power, Global Capital and the Housing Bubble*, Cornell University Press, 2009.

15. D. Awrey, 'Toward a Supply-Side Theory of Financial Innovation', *Journal of Comparative Economics*, vol. 41:2, 2013, p. 401.

16. T. Piketty, *Capital in the Twenty-First Century*, Harvard University Press, 2014.

17. TheCityUK, 2013.

Notes on Chapter 2

18. In the US, AUM increased from around 50 per cent of GDP to around 240 per cent of GDP. In the UK, the same trend has unfolded in a much shorter space of time since 1980. A. Haldane, 'The Age of Asset Management', speech at London Business School, 4 April 2014, www.bankofen gland.co.uk/speech/2014/the-age-of-asset-management.

19. P. A. Samuelson, 'Proof That Properly Anticipated Prices Fluctuate Randomly', in *The World Scientific Handbook of Futures Markets* (World Scientific Handbook in Financial Economics Series), World Scientific, 2015, ch. 2, p. 41.

20. Reuters, 'Global financial market losses $50 trillion: ADB study', 9 March 2009, www.reuters.com/article/us-financial-adb/global-financial -market-losses-50-trillion-adb-study-idUSTRE5281FN20090309.

Chapter 3. Be First, Be Smarter and Cheat

1. Being first, John Tuld orders his troops to fire-sell the bank's toxic products, shifting them on to any clients, colleagues or competitors, using any tricks in the book.

2. W. Frame and L. White, 'Empirical Studies of Financial Innovation: Lots of Talk, Little Action?', Working Paper 2002–12, Federal Reserve Bank of Atlanta, 2002.

3. S. Polillo, *Conservatives vs Wildcats: A Sociology of Financial Conflict*, Stanford University Press, 2013.

4. 'Stars of the Junkyard', *Economist*, 21 October 2010, www.economist .com/briefing/2010/10/21/stars-of-the-junkyard.

5. W. Cohan, 'Michael Milken invented the modern junk bond, went to prison, and then became one of the most respected people on Wall Street', Business Insider, 2 May 2017, http://uk.businessinsider.com/michael-mil ken-life-story-2017-5?r=US&IR=T.

6. 'Stars of the Junkyard', *Economist*.

7. Cohan, 'Michael Milken invented the modern junk bond'.

8. 'Stars of the Junkyard', *Economist*.

9. Cohan, 'Michael Milken invented the modern junk bond'.

10. Insights for this section come from the best story written about the role of Ranieri personally and Salomon Brothers as an institution: Mi-

Notes on Chapter 3

chael Lewis's *Liar's Poker: Two Cities, True Greed*, Hodder and Stoughton, 1989.

11. T. Piskorski, A. Seru and J. Witkin, 'Asset Quality Misrepresentation by Financial Intermediaries: Evidence from RMBS Market', Kreisman Working Paper Series in Housing Law and Policy, No. 9, University of Chicago Law School, 2013.

12. So argued Donald Hawthorne, a partner at Axinn Veltrop & Harkrider LLP, who has represented monoline insurers and RMBS investors in suits against mortgage originators, including Countrywide, relating to mortgage securities. Source: D. Ingram and P. Rudegeair, 'U.S. accuses Bank of America of mortgage-backed securities fraud', Reuters, 6 August 2013, https://uk.reuters.com/article/us-bofa-justice-idUSBRE9750ZU20130806.

13. Press Association, 'Barclays agrees to pay $2bn to settle US fraud case', *Guardian*, 29 March 2018, www.theguardian.com/business/2018/mar/29/barclays-agrees-to-pay-2bn-to-settle-us-case-justice-department-mortgage-backed-securities.

14. M. Arnold, 'RBS settles DoJ fraud claims over mortgage-backed securities', *Financial Times*, 26 October 2017, www.ft.com/content/2231f092-f991-3eef-9ebe-4a46ed6ddf9f.

15. 'Banks paid $321 billion in fines since financial crisis: BCG', Reuters, 2 March 2017, www.reuters.com/article/us-banks-fines/banks-paid-321-billion-in-fines-since-financial-crisis-bcg-idUSKBN1692Y2.

16. S. Tully, 'Lewie Ranieri wants to fix the mortgage mess', *Fortune*, 9 December 2009, http://archive.fortune.com/2009/12/08/real_estate/lewie_ranieri_mortgages.fortune/index.htm.

17. SIFMA, Bonds Outstanding, www.sifma.org/resources/research/bond-chart/.

18. By far the best story of the CDS and the work of the team is Gillian Tett's *Fool's Gold: How Unrestrained Greed Corrupted a Dream, Shattered Global Markets and Unleashed a Catastrophe*, Abacus, 2009.

19. F. Norris, 'Naked truth on default swaps', *The New York Times*, 10 May 2010, www.nytimes.com/2010/05/21/business/economy/21norris.html?mtrref=www.google.com.

20. Ibid.

21. H. Hu, 'Reform the credit default swap market to reign in abuses', *Financial Times*, 24 February 2019, www.ft.com/content/1fcd2f34-2e14 -11e9-80d2-7b637a9e1ba1.

22. A. Davidson, 'How AIG fell apart', Reuters, 18 September 2008, www .reuters.com/article/us-how-aig-fell-apart-idUSMAR85972720080918.

23. Ibid.

24. Ibid.

25. Ibid.

26. J. Giannone, 'AIG bailout good for banks while investors bleed', Reuters, 11 March 2009, www.reuters.com/article/us-aig-bailout-sb-idUSTRE 52A0TP20090311.

27. 'Credit derivatives: the great untangling', *Economist*, 6 November 2008, www.economist.com/briefing/2008/11/06/the-great-untangling.

28. H. Minsky, *Stabilizing an Unstable Economy*, Yale University Press, 1986, p. 346.

29. J. Hosters, 'Joseph Schumpeter and His Legacy in Innovation Studies', *Knowledge, Technology, & Policy*, vol. 18:3, 2005, pp. 20–37. J. A. Schumpeter, 'The Influence of Protective Tariffs on the Industrial Development of the United States', in *Proceedings of the Academy of Political Science*, May 1940, pp. 2–7.

30. M. Lavoie, *Introduction to Post-Keynesian Economics*, Palgrave Macmillan, 2009.

31. It would take years for lawyers to disentangle the CDS exposure of Lehman Brothers and many other firms that failed in 2007–9.

32. D. Newman, 'Exploring 5 Trends Driving the Fintech Revolution', *Forbes*, 3 July 2018.

PART TWO. 'NO CONFLICT, NO INTEREST'

Chapter 4. Dead Souls at the Royal Bank of Scotland

1. Letter to Treasury Select Committee, House of Commons, London, 28 January 2018, BankConfidential, TSC/BC/WB/10118, https://bankcon fidential.com/wp-content/uploads/2018/02/TSC-Final-letter-1-1.pdf.

2. The above details were revealed by BankConfidential, an organization set up specifically to assist whistleblowers in the RBS Group and other banks willing to report abuse in their institutions.

3. Promontory Financial Group, 'RBS Group Treatment of the SME Customers Referred to the Global Restructuring Group', report prepared for the Financial Conduct Authority, September 2016.

4. T. Edmonds, 'Treatment of SMEs by RBS Global Restructuring Group', Debate Pack, House of Commons Library, 16 January 2018.

5. Ibid.

6. Clifford Chance LLP, 2011, 'Independent Review of the Central Allegation Made by Dr Lawrence Tomlinson in Banks' Lending Practices: Treatment of Businesses in Distress', 11 April 2014, www.rbs.com/content/dam /rbs_com/rbs/Documents/News/2014/04/Clifford-Chance-Independent -Review.pdf.

7. C. Binham, 'RBS unit memo told staff to let clients "hang themselves"', *Financial Times*, 17 January 2018.

8. I. Fraser, 'A Short History of RBS's Global Restructuring Group', Ian Fraser blog, 17 June 2012, www.ianfraser.org/has-rbs-become-a-rogue -institution/.

9. A. Verity, 'The hotel that RBS took...and sold to RBS', BBC Business News, 18 April 2018, www.bbc.com/news/business-43486731.

10. Easter quoted in T. Bristow, 'Four hotels, an £8m firm, all gone – one Norfolk hotelier's battle with RBS', *Eastern Daily Press*, 21 March 2018, www.edp24.co.uk/business/hotelier-david-easter-rbs-grg-turnaround -norfolk-1-5443669; https://senecabanking.co.uk/tales-from-the-global-rest ructuring-group/.

11. PWC, 'Arlington Place Hotel Limited – in Administration', The Joint Administrators' Final Progress Report for the period from 11 July 2013 to 2 January 2014, PWC, 2 January 2014, p. 5.

12. Hansard, 'Treasury Committee: Oral Evidence: RBS' Global Restructuring Group and Its Treatment of SMEs', HC 737, 30 January 2018, http://data.parliament.uk/writtenevidence/committeeevidence.svc /evidencedocument/treasury-committee/rbs-global-restructuring-group -and-its-treatment-of-smes/oral/77683.html.

13. Ibid.

14. I. Fraser, 'My nightmare 10-year battle for RBS damages: businessman in landmark court victory backs campaign for safeguards', *Financial Mail on Sunday*, 28 October 2017.

Notes on Chapter 4

15. I. Fraser, 'RBS executives seem to think they're above the law', Ian Fraser blog, 16 December 2010.

16. J. Treanor 'RBS facing £400m bill to compensate small business customers', *Guardian*, 8 November 2016, www.theguardian.com/business/2016/nov/08/rbs-facing-400m-bill-to-compensate-small-business-customers.

17. Ibid.; also I. Fraser, *Shredded: Inside RBS, the Bank That Broke Britain*, Birlinn, 2014.

18. Edmonds, 'Treatment of SMEs by RBS Global Restructuring Group'.

19. L. Boyce, '"I worked at RBS during the financial crisis – and sales pressure is now ten times worse": dozens more whistleblowers step forward to tell of bank misery', This is Money, 4 August 2016, www.thisismoney.co.uk/money/saving/article-3712765/Dozens-RBS-staff-tell-hard-sales-pressure-branches.html.

20. N. Megaw, 'RBS ranked UK's least popular bank', *Financial Times*, 15 August 2018.

21. C. Binham, 'MPs slam "regulatory black hole" for bank lending to small business', *Financial Times*, 26 October 2018, www.ft.com/content/551fb48a-d875-11e8-a854-33d6f82e62f8.

Chapter 5. 'Our People Are Our Greatest Asset'

1. M. Levine, 'Abacus CDO bites Goldman back', Bloomberg, 26 September 2018, www.bloomberg.com/opinion/articles/2018-09-26/abacus-cdo-bites-goldman-back.

2. Goldman Sachs, Consent of Defendant Goldman, Sachs & Co., *SEC v. Goldman Sachs & Co.*, 790 F. Supp. 2d 147 (SDNY 2011) (No. 10-CV-3229), 2010 WL 2779309.

3. Note 3 in SEC, Complaint, Litigation Release, 2010, www.sec.gov/litigation/complaints/2010/comp-pr2010-59.pdf.

4. In legal terms, the case against Goldman was not watertight. If the bank had focused on the detail of the defence and, more importantly, on the aspects of the structured deal, it could have won the case.

5. E. Rosenbaum, 'Goldman Sachs stock: buy, sell or hold?', TheStreet, 20 April 2010, www.thestreet.com/story/10728591/1/goldman-sachs-stock-buy-sell-or-hold.html.

6. The case against Fabrice Tourre, a former Goldman trader who was found liable for defrauding investors, was not part of the settlement. See www.reuters.com/article/us-goldmansachs-sec-tourre-idUSKBN0E72 JG20140527.

7. Levine, 'Abacus CDO bites Goldman back'. Italics in the original.

8. Still, the overall role of the section within Goldman Sachs should not be exaggerated. Although CDO and structured product trading was responsible for almost half of the mortgage desk's 2006 revenue of $1bn, this was a small portion of Goldman Sachs's overall revenue of $38bn (B. McLean and J. Nocera, *All the Devils Are Here: Unmasking the Men Who Blew Up the World*, Viking, 2010).

9. www.goldmansachs.com/who-we-are/people-and-culture/index .html?view=mobile.

Chapter 6. 'A Simple Premise'

1. M. Egan, '5,300 Wells Fargo employees fired over 2 million phony accounts', CNN Business, 2016, https://money.cnn.com/2016/09/08/inves ting/wells-fargo-created-phony-accounts-bank-fees/index.html.

2. Ibid.

3. M. Levine, 'Wells Fargo opened a couple million fake accounts', Bloomberg, 9 September 2016.

4. P. Rucker, 'Exclusive: Wells Fargo faces sanctions for auto insurance payouts – sources', Reuters, 15 March 2018, www.reuters.com/art icle/us-wells-fargo-accounts-auto-exclusive/exclusive-wells-fargo-faces -sanctions-for-auto-insurance-payouts-sources-idUSKCN1GR0G3.

5. E. Glazer, 'Whistleblowers detail Wells Fargo wealth management woes', *Wall Street Journal*, 27 July 2018.

6. Ibid.

7. Ibid.

8. Ibid.

9. Ibid.

10. www.wellsfargo.com/about/corporate/vision-and-values/.

11. C. Binham, 'MPs slam "regulatory black hole" for bank lending to small business', *Financial Times*, 26 October 2018, www.ft.com/content /551fb48a-d875-11e8-a854-33d6f82e62f8.

PART THREE. HOSTICIDE

1. The rise of Goldman during the crisis generated wide-ranging conspiracy theories. People did not fail to notice how well Goldman's alumni were entrenched in government: Duncan Niederauer in the NYSE; Joshua Bolten, the president's chief of staff; Robert Rubin, the US Treasury Secretary under Bill Clinton; Robert Zoellick at the World Bank; and Hank Paulson at the Treasury. For more on the political connections of the financiers see, among others: Jeff Madrick's *Age of Greed: The Triumph of Finance and the Decline of America, 1970 to the Present*, Vintage Books, 2012; Gillian Tett's *Fool's Gold: How Unrestrained Greed Corrupted a Dream, Shattered Global Markets and Unleashed a Catastrophe*, Abacus, 2009; and Rana Foroohar's *Makers and Takers: How Wall Street Destroyed Main Street*, Crown Business, 2017.

Chapter 7. Who Let the Bear Down?

1. ' America's Most Admired Companies', *Fortune*, 2007.

2. The Wall Street journalist Kate Kelly described the bank as 'lean, scrappy, and hungry for profits'. One of our interviewees said of Bear simply: 'Those guys were criminals'.

3. Kate Kelly, *Street Fighters: The Last 72 Hours of Bear Stearns, the Toughest Firm on Wall Street*, Portfolio, 2009, pp. 25–6.

4. The prize winners found a mathematical way to price predicted volatility in the market. In a very short time of its ascent, LTCM became a legend. Everything about it – the pedigree of its staff, methods, approach – appeared to prove that a scientific approach to understanding risk in finance can bring material superprofits: leveraged at 25:1, LTCM generated 40 per cent returns for its clients.

5. Prime brokerage services include securities lending, leverage operations and cash management. These types of services are typically provided by large banks and revolve around facilitating the diverse trading operations of large financial institutions.

6. The following institutions contributed $300m: Bankers Trust, Barclays, Chase, Credit Suisse First Boston, Deutsche Bank, Goldman Sachs, Merrill Lynch, J. P. Morgan, Morgan Stanley, Salomon Smith Barney and

UBS. Société Générale chipped in $125m; Paribas and Crédit Agricole $100m each.

7. Jimmy Cayne's move also increased uncertainty about this deal as Bear acted as LTCM's clearing house and knew more than anyone about LTCM's financial position.

8. William D. Cohan, *House of Cards: How Wall Street's Gamblers Broke Capitalism*, Allen Lane, 2009, pp. 244–53.

9. Ibid., p. 321.

10. The institution filed for bankruptcy on 2 April 2007 (Cohan, *House of Cards*, pp. 317, 320).

11. Ibid., p. 320.

12. Ibid., p. 327.

13. Ibid., p. 378.

14. In November 2007 the *Wall Street Journal* published an article criticizing Bear's CEO. It accused James Cayne of playing bridge and smoking pot instead of focusing on saving the company (K. Kelly, 'Bear CEO's handling of crisis raises issues', *Wall Street Journal*, 1 November 2007, www.wsj.com/articles/SB119387369474078336). Although Cayne fought back against the allegations in a memo to Bear staff, the publication further damaged Bear Stearns's reputation (K. Amadeo, 'Bear Stearns, Its Collapse, and Bailout', The Balance, 8 October 2018). See also https://dealbook.nytimes.com/2007/11/02/the-bear-stearns-memo-cayne-speaks/.

15. Kelly, *Street Fighters*, p. 15.

16. Cohan, *House of Cards*, p. 11.

17. R. Boyd, 'The last days of Bear Stearns', *Fortune*, 31 March 2008.

18. It could never be determined, which bank, although it was speculated that it was Deutsche Bank (Cohan, *House of Cards*, p. 16).

19. Boyd, 'The last days of Bear Stearns'.

20. Ibid.

21. Kelly, *Street Fighters*, p. 14.

22. Cohan, *House of Cards*, p. 23.

23. Run by a former Bear Stearns employee, John Paulson.

24. B. Burrough, 'Bringing Down Bear Stearns', *Vanity Fair*, 30 June 2008, www.vanityfair.com/news/2008/08/bear_stearns200808-2.

25. Ibid.

26. Goldman Sachs's credit derivatives group sent its hedge fund clients an email announcing it would no longer step in for them on Bear derivatives deals. 'I was astounded when I got the [Goldman] e-mail,' says Kyle Bass of Hayman Capital. He had a colleague call Goldman to see if it was a mistake. 'It wasn't,' says Bass, who is a former Bear salesman. 'Goldman told Wall Street that they were done with Bear, that there was [effectively] too much risk. That was the end for them', http://archive.fortune.com/2008/03/28/magazines/fortune/boyd_bear.fortune/index.htm.

27. Cohan, *House of Cards*, pp. 27–8.

28. Kelly, *Street Fighters*, pp. 15–16.

29. L. Chincarini, *The Crisis of Crowding: Quant Copycats, Ugly Models, and the New Crash Normal*, John Wiley and Sons, 2012, p. 150.

30. Boyd, 'The last days of Bear Stearns'.

31. Burrough, 'Bringing Down Bear Stearns'.

32. Ibid.

33. Paul Friedman, managing director and in charge of refinancing operations (Fixed Income Division) recalls that 'the loss of confidence had three related consequences: prime brokerage clients withdrew their cash and unencumbered securities at a rapid and increasing rate; repo market lenders declined to roll over or renew repo loans, even when the loans were supported by high-quality collateral such as agency securities; and counterparties to non-simultaneous settlements of foreign exchange trades refused to pay until Bear Stearns paid first. Although this loss of confidence in Bear Stearns was unwarranted given the firm's strong capital position and substantial liquidity, it resulted in a rapid flight of capital from the firm that could not be survived.' Friedman concluded in front of the US Financial Crisis Inquiry Commission: 'In retrospect, I do not believe that there was anything that Bear Stearns could have done differently with respect to its funding model that would have prevented this run on the bank' (FCIC, 'Financial Crisis Inquiry Report').

34. Ibid. Due to Bear's status as a non-depository institution it could not have received the central bank loan directly. It was later investigated whether the Fed's indirect involvement was legitimate.

35. Amadeo, 'Bearn Stearns, Its Collapse, and Bailout'.

36. Ibid.

37. R. Peston, 'How hedge funds sunk Bear Stearns', BBC News, 14 March 2008.

38. A. Clark, 'Former Bear Stearns boss Jimmy Cayne blames conspiracy for bank's collapse', *Guardian*, 5 May 2010.

39. K. Kelly and S. Craig, 'Goldman is queried about Bear's fall', *Wall Street Journal*, 16 July 2008. Goldman representatives insisted on multiple occasions that their actions were never prompted by ill intentions (Cohan, *House of Cards*, p. 28).

40. Z. Goldfarb, 'Former Bear Stearns executives blame collapse on "self-fulfilling prophecy"', *Washington Post*, 6 May 2010.

41. K. Kelly, 'EC will scour Bear trading data', *Wall Street Journal*, 28 May 2008.

42. Kelly, *Street Fighters*, p. 21.

43. Burrough, 'Bringing Down Bear Stearns'.

Chapter 8. What goes around comes around

1. P. Augar, *The Death of Gentlemanly Capitalism: The Rise and Fall of London's Investment Banks*, Penguin Books, 2008.

2. I. Fraser, *Shredded: Inside RBS, the Bank That Broke Britain*, Birlinn, 2014, pp. 23–4.

3. Ibid., p. 52.

4. Ibid., p. 77.

5. Ibid.

6. Ibid., p. 94.

7. Ibid., p. 96.

8. 'Scots on the Rocks', *Economist*, 25 February 2010.

9. Fraser, *Shredded*, p. 239.

10. Ibid.

11. Ibid., p. 243

12. Ibid., p. 264.

13. While this was a reasonable safety measure for the Dutch regulators aiming to secure the amount of €1.025tn on ABN's balance sheet, the requirement put RBS in a risky regulatory straitjacket.

14. Fraser, *Shredded*, pp. 249–50.

15. Ibid., p. 256.

16. Ibid., p. 259, and I. Fraser, 'Do Merrill Lynch bankers know no shame?', Ian Fraser blog, 23 January 2009.

17. RBS bought a 1 per cent stake in Santander, and Santander bought a 9.9 per cent stake in RBS and granted all its voting rights to RBS.

18. Fraser, *Shredded*, p. 47.

19. 'Emilio Botin', Bloomberg Businessweek, 17 June 2002.

20. E. Robinson, and M. Montijano, 'Santander's Ana Botin has something to prove', Bloomberg, 23 November 2015.

21. 'They became accustomed to sharing ideas with Santander's directors Juan Rodriguez Inciarte and Emilio Botín... One consensual view that emerged from these sessions was that the banking sector consolidation was going to accelerate and any bank that failed to make acquisitions would become a take-over target itself' (Fraser, *Shredded*, p. 50).

22. Ibid. Santander had acquired ABN's Brazilian and Italian subsidiaries and had plans to resell the Italian unit immediately to Banco Monte dei Paschi di Siena.

23. Fraser, *Shredded*, p. 261.

24. Ibid.

25. 'The banker the credit crisis couldn't touch', *Independent*, 27 July 2008, www.independent.co.uk/news/business/analysis-and-features/the-banker-the-credit-crisis-couldnt-touch-878002.html.

26. Fraser, *Shredded*, p. 349.

27. J. Pickard and S. Goff, 'Santander can bid for RBS business branches', *Financial Times*, 1 November 2009.

28. Ibid.

29. 'Scots on the Rocks', *Economist*.

30. Fraser, *Shredded*, p. 252.

31. A. Seager, L. Elliot and J. Kollewe, 'Barclays admits borrowing hundreds of millions at Bank's emergency rate', *Guardian*, 31 August 2007.

32. Ibid.

33. The circumstances of this arrangement became the subject of an investigation by the Financial Conduct Authority and the Serious Fraud Office (D. Schäfer et al., 'Barclays in Qatar loan probe', *Financial Times*, 30 January 2013). In 2018 the UK court had thrown the case out.

34. H.Wilson, P. Aldrick and K. Ahmed, 'RBS investigation: Chapter 2 – the ABN Amro takeover', *Telegraph*, 11 December 2011.

35. 'RBS and Barclays should both be getting the jitters', 'Comment', *Telegraph*, 28 July 2007.

36. J. Werdingier, 'Barclays withdraws bid to take over ABN-Amro', *The New York Times*, 6 October 2007.

Chapter 9. Beware Good Advice

1. P. Jenkins and L. Noonan, 'How Deutsche Bank's high-stakes gamble went wrong', *Financial Times*, 9 November 2017.

2. Soon after his appointment he said: 'I have no idea why I was offered a contract with a bonus in it because I promise you I will not work any harder or any less hard in any year, in any day because someone is going to pay me more or less.' Ibid.

3. Ibid.

4. There were 'retention payments' for 5,522 'mission-critical people'. 'It was probably one of the most difficult decisions we took,' says one board member.

5. In many respects the bank had outgrown Iceland and many of its activities were conducted from Britain. Most investment banking operations were conducted in London, many clients were British-based and, in 2008 at least, about €3.5bn (£3bn) poured into KSF from UK savers in the shape of online deposits in its high-interest online account Kaupthing Edge.

6. G. Robinson, 'Kaupthing: We're not – repeat NOT – desperate', *Financial Times*, 'Alphaville', 5 March 2008.

7. In Icelandic: www.mbl.is/media/00/1200.pdf.

8. Executive summary of the SIC report is available in English at www.rna.is/media/skjol/RNAvefKafli2Enska.pdf.

9. Sigrún Davídsdóttir, 8 December 2015 at 11.57 p.m. (Sigrún Davíðsdóttir, undated, 'What is Deutsche Bank hiding in Iceland?', Sigrún Davíðsdóttir's Icelog, http://uti.is/?s=deutsche).

10. Ibid.

11. Ibid.

12. S. Bowers, 'London business figures embroiled in Kaupthing fraud investigation', *Guardian*, 6 June 2010.

13. Deutsche Bank, Annual Report, 2016, p. 369. SPV Proceedings refers to the two offshore companies, Chesterfield and Partridge.

14. 'Deutsche bank zahlt 450 Millionen im Kaupthing-Vergleich', *Manager Magazin*, 22 March 2017, www.manager-magazin.de/unternehmen /banken/deutsche-bank-offenbar-450-millionen-im-kaupthing-vergleich -gezahlt-a-1139859.html (in German]; Deutsche Bank, Annual Report, 2016, p. 369.

15. 'Beide Asien-Finanzchefs beurlaubt', Handelsblatt, 19 May 2015 (in German only).

PART FOUR. THE BIG, THE BAD AND THE CRYPTO

Chapter 10. The Big

1. T. Braithwaite, 'Dimon warns breaking up JPMorgan would hurt US financial power', *Financial Times*. 14 January 2015.

2. M. Arnold et al., 'Banking M&A: the quest to create a European champion', *Financial Times*, 11 July 2018.

3. N. Ranawake, 'There is no debate; the country needs bigger and stronger banks', *Daily FT*, 29 June 2018.

4. M. O'Hara and W. Shaw, 'Deposit Insurance and Wealth Effects: The Value of Being 'Too Big to Fail', *Journal of Finance*, vol. 45, 1990, pp. 1587–1600.

5. D. P. Morgan and K. J. Stiroh, 'Too Big to Fail after All These Years (SSRN Scholarly Paper No. ID 813967), Social Science Research Network, Rochester, NY, 2005.

6. A. Haldane, 'On Being the Right Size', speech at the Institute of Economic Affairs, 22nd Annual Series, The 2012 Beesley Lectures, at the Institute of Directors, London, 25 October 2012, www.bis.org/review/r121030d.pdf.

7. M. J. Roe, 'Structural Corporate Degradation Due to Too-Big-to-Fail Finance', *University of Pennsylvania Law Review*, vol. 162, 2014, pp. 1419–64.

8. A post-2009 rule that requires banks to prepare 'living wills' – documents that stipulate in advance how the institution would raise funds in a crisis and how their operations could be dismantled after a collapse.

9. S. Nasiripour, 'Largest banks likely profited by borrowing from Federal Reserve, lending to Federal Government', Huffington Post, 26 April 2011.

10. Ibid.

11. D. Wheelock, 'Too Big to Fail: The Pros and Cons of Breaking Up Big Banks', Regional Economist, St Louis Fed, October 2012.

12. W. Harrison, 'In defence of big banks', The New York Times, 22 August 2012.

13. G. J. Benston, W. C. Hunter, and L. D. Wall, 'Motivations for Bank Mergers and Acquisitions: Enhancing the Deposit Insurance Put Option versus Earnings Diversification', Journal of Money, Credit and Banking, vol. 27, 1995, pp. 777–88.

14. E. Brewer and J. Jagtiani, 'How Much Did Banks Pay to Become Too-Big-To-Fail and to Become Systemically Important?', Journal of Financial Services Research, vol. 43, 2013, pp. 1–35.

15. Moody's, 'Danièle Nouy of ECB on Consolidation in European Banking Sector', 27 September 2017, www.moodysanalytics.com/regulatory-news /sept-27-daniele-nouy-of-ecb-on-consolidation-in-european-banking -sector.

16. P. Larsen, 'Lever again', Reuters, 27 December 2017, www.break ingviews.com/features/regulators-will-drive-next-wave-of-eu-bank -mergers/.

17. F. Fiordelisi, 'Why Do Banks Merge?', in: Mergers and Acquisitions in European Banking, Palgrave Macmillan Studies in Banking and Financial Institutions, Palgrave Macmillan, 2009, pp. 48–84; D. Focarelli, F. Panetta and C. Salleo, 'Why Do Banks Merge?', Journal of Money, Credit and Banking, vol. 34, 2002, pp. 1047–66.

18. G. Morgentson, 'A bank too big to jail', The New York Times, 15 July 2016, www.nytimes.com/2016/07/17/business/a-bank-too-big-to-jail .html.

19. A. Monaghan, '"Too big to fail" risks growing in asset management', Guardian, 4 April 2014, www.theguardian.com/business/2014/apr/04/as set-management-risks-bailout-rising-warns-bank-of-england.

Notes on Chapter 11

Chapter 11. The Bad

1. According to investment guides, 'there are no laws or regulations in the Cayman Islands that specifically regulate OTC equity derivatives transactions between dealers, nor is there a regulatory authority specifically responsible for such regulation', https://gettingthedealthrough.com/area/85/jurisdiction/59/equity-derivatives-cayman-islands/.

2. The rating depends on the methodology adopted.

3. R. Mason, 'Bankrupt Cayman Islands to get £38m bail-out', *Telegraph*, 30 September 2009, www.telegraph.co.uk/finance/financialcrisis/6248284/Bankrupt-Cayman-Islands-to-get-38m-bail-out.html.

4. US Senate, 'Abuse of Structured Products', Majority and Minority Staff Report, Permanent Subcommittee on Investigations, 22 July 2014 Hearing, p. 3.

5. Ibid., p. 2.

6. Ibid., p. 3.

7. Ibid. Deutsche and Barclays were not alone. It is generally believed that the first basket option structure had been designed by the Royal Bank of Canada (RBC) in 1996. The RBC marketed a basket option structure using a derivative option on a managed trading account to circumvent the Canadian leverage restrictions of Regulation T (US Senate, 2014, p. 1855, footnote). Similar ruses were often used to minimize exposure to withholding taxes, and have been a popular loophole exploited by hedge funds since the 1990s (L. Lopez, 'The IRS is getting serious about cracking down on another cherished hedge fund tax loophole', Business Insider, 1 July 2013).

Chapter 12. The Crypto

1. At the time, Russia did not have a law on securities fraud.

2. 'How MMM Works?', https://bitcointalk.org/index.php?topic=77276.0.

3. M. Carney, 'The Promise of FinTech – Something New under the Sun?', speech at the Bank of England, 25 January 2017, www.bankofengland.co.uk/speech/2017/the-promise-of-fintech-something-new-under-the-sun.

Notes on Chapter 12

4. European Commission, 'What is Fintech?', https://ec.europa.eu /info/business-economy-euro/banking-and-finance/fintech_en.

5. Back in the late 1950s the Eurodollar market, a market that emerged in London almost by accident, has swiftly plugged a hole in the entire postwar regulatory regime known as the Bretton Woods system.

6. So dubbed by the University of California–Irvine law professor Omri Marian.

7. O. Bateman, 'Bitcoin might make tax havens obsolete', Motherboard, *Vice*, 22 June 2016, https://motherboard.vice.com/en_us/article /wnxzpy/bitcoin-might-make-tax-havens-obsolete.

8. D. Ketchum, '15 biggest crowdfunding scams and failures of all time', Go Banking Rates, 14 March 2018, www.gobankingrates.com/making -money/business/biggest-crowdfunding-scams-failures/.

9. 'Fed researchers compare P2P lending to subprime mortgages', Finextra, 10 November 2017, www.finextra.com/newsarticle/31322/fed -researchers-compare-p2p-lending-to-subprime-mortgages.

10. https://en.wikipedia.org/wiki/Lending_Club.

11. P. Rudegeair, 'LendingClub CEO fired over faulty loans', *Wall Street Journal*, 9 May 2016, www.wsj.com/articles/lendingclub-ceo-resigns-over -sales-review-1462795070.

12. M. Erman and H. Somerville, 'LendingClub says ex-CEO took loans to boost volumes', Reuters, 28 June 2016, www.reuters.com/article/us -lendingclub-ceo-idUSKCN0ZE13Q.

13. 'FTC charges Lending Club with deceiving consumers', FTC press release, 25 April 2018, www.ftc.gov/news-events/press-releases/2018/04 /ftc-charges-lending-club-deceiving-consumers-0.

14. G. Wildau and Y. Jia, 'Collapse of Chinese peer-to-peer lenders sparks investor flight', *Financial Times*, 22 July 2018, www.ft.com/content /75e75628-8b27-11e8-bf9e-8771d5404543.

15. I. Kaminska, 'Fintech's security/access paradox problem', *Financial Times*, 'Alphaville', 3 October 2016, https://ftalphaville.ft.com/2016 /10/03/2176471/fintechs-securityaccess-paradox-problem/.

16. Until 2013 the so-called Silk Road (DEF) was the primary e-commerce platform on the dark web. After its founder, Dread Pirate Roberts,

or Ross Ulbricht, went down, it was succeeded by AlphaBay and many other dark marketplaces. Dread Pirate Roberts is now in prison serving a life sentence. The authorities still can't get their hands on most of his bitcoins.

17. L. Katz, 'Criminals may ditch bitcoin for Litecoin, Dash, study says', Bloomberg, 8 February 2018, www.bloomberg.com/news/articles /2018-02-08/criminals-are-ditching-bitcoin-for-litecoin-and-dash-study -says.

18. Bateman, 'Bitcoin might make tax havens obsolete'.

19. Ibid.

20. Conducted in January 2018. (Source: J. Wieczner, 'Bitcoin investors aren't paying their cryptocurrency taxes', *Fortune*, 13 February 2018, http:// fortune.com/2018/02/13/bitcoin-cryptocurrency-tax-taxes/).

21. Ibid.

22. Ibid.

23. Ibid.

24. E. Kelso, 'New study: 80% of ICOs are scams, only 8% reach an exchange', Bitcoin.com, 28 March 2018, https://news.bitcoin.com/80-of-icos -are-scams-only-8-reach-an-exchange/.

25. CNN, 'ICO scams have raised more than $1 billion, report claims', 19 May 2018, www.ccn.com/ico-scams-have-raised-more-than-1-billion-re port-claims/.

26. H. Partz, 'SEC launches mock ICO to show investors warning signs of fraud', Coin Telegraph, 16 May 2018, https://cointelegraph.com/news /sec-launches-mock-ico-to-show-investors-warning-signs-of-fraud.

27. I. Kaminska, 'Fintech as a gateway for criminal enterprise', *Financial Times*, 'Alphaville', 12 January 2018, https://ftalphaville.ft.com/2018/01/12 /2197610/fintech-as-a-gateway-for-criminal-enterprise.

PART FIVE. CONCLUSION

Chapter 13. Old News

1. R. McKinnon, *Money and Capital in Economic Development*, Brookings Institution, 1973.

2. Named so after senator Ferdinand Pecora, who was the fourth and final person to lead the 1932–4 Senate Committee on Banking and Cur-

rency investigation into the abusive practices in banking and finance. Pecora expanded the remit and scope of the investigation to get to the core of the dynamics that had brought about the 1929 crash.

3. Senate Committee on Banking and Currency, 'The Pecora Report: The 1934 Report on the Practices of Stock Exchanges from the Pecora Commission', US Senate, Report No. 1455, June 2009 [1934], pp. 9, 30, www .senate.gov/artandhistory/history/common/.../pdf/Pecora_FinalReport .pdf.

4. Ibid.

5. Ibid.

6. Ibid. p. 9.

7. Ibid., p. 31.

8. Ibid., p. 81.

9. Ibid., p. 85.

10. Ibid., p. 87.

11. Ibid., pp. 110ff.

12. Ibid., p. 113.

13. Ibid., p. 360.

14. Ibid., p. 363.

15. Ibid., p. 373.

16. Ibid., p. 381.

17. Ibid., p. 384.

18. Ibid., p. 214.

19. Ibid., p. 4.

20. Section 4 of the Federal Reserve Act.

21. M. Price and P. Schroeder, 'Trump's consumer financial chief disbands key advisory boards', Reuters, 6 June 2018, www.reuters.com /article/us-usa-cfpb-boards/trumps-consumer-financial-chief-disbands -key-advisory-boards-idUSKCN1J22PN.

22. M. Wolf, 'Banking remains far too undercapitalised for comfort', *Financial Times*, 21 September 2017, www.ft.com/content/9dd43a1a-9d49 -11e7-8cd4-932067fbf946.

23. L. Noonan and P. Jenkins, 'JPMorgan: defying attempts to end "too big to fail"', *Financial Times*, 12 September 2018, www.ft.com/content /0eebc7de-b4de-11e8-b3ef-799c8613f4a1.

Notes on Chapter 13

24. A. Cuomo, 'No Rhyme or Reason: The Heads I Win, Tails You Lose Bank Bonus Culture', 2009, p. 2.

25. Ibid., p. 5.

26. I. Kottasowa, '9 trillion and counting: how central banks are still flooding the world with money', CNN Business, 9 September 2016, https://money.cnn.com/2016/09/08/news/economy/central-banks-printed-nine-trillion/index.html.

27. K. Darrah, 'The QE reversal', World Finance, 26 April 2018, www.worldfinance.com/banking/the-qe-reversal.

28. P. Donohoe, 'How often is the "Single Malt" tax loophole used? The government is finding out', The Journal, 15 November 2017, www.thejournal.ie/single-malt-tax-evasion-3698512-Nov2017.

29. R. Griffin et al., 'How Azerbaijan's biggest bank used Dublin on way to default', *Irish Times*, 19 June 2017, www.irishtimes.com/business/financial-services/how-azerbaijan-s-biggest-bank-used-dublin-on-way-to-default-1.3124981.

30. In 2014 the most profitable investment and commercial bank in the UK, J. P. Morgan Securities Plc, had $2.6bn (£1.75bn) in profits but paid no tax according to its country-by-country report (CBCR). J. P. Morgan had a UK tax liability of $524m, but the sum was offset by foreign tax credits, overpayments in previous periods and 'the benefit of other available tax reliefs' (H. Austin, 'Five of world's biggest investment banks pay no UK corporation tax', *Independent*, 23 December 2015, www.independent.co.uk/news/business/news/five-of-worlds-biggest-investment-banks-pay-no-uk-corporation-tax-a6783716.html). Overall corporation tax has fallen as a proportion of the total tax paid by the financial services sector in the UK from 40.8 per cent in 2007 to only 19.8 per cent in 2015 (M. Arnold et al., 'Banks pay lowest proportion of tax since before financial crisis', *Financial Times*, 4 December 2015, www.ft.com/content/1414b394-99dc-11e5-987b-d6cdef1b205c).

31. M. Aubrey, and T. Dauphin, 'Opening the Vaults: The Use of Tax Havens by Europe's Biggest Banks.' Oxfam, 2017.

32. Jessica Fino, 'UK Banks Make £9bn in Profits in Tax Havens', *Economia*, 27 March 2017, https://economia.icaew.com/news/march-2017/uk-banks-hold-9bn-in-profits-in-tax-havens.

Chapter 14. So What?

1. Senate Committee on Banking and Currency, 'The Pecora Report: The 1934 Report on the Practices of Stock Exchanges from the Pecora Commission', US Senate, Report No. 1455, June 2009 [1934], p. 31, www.senate.gov/artandhistory/history/common/.../pdf/Pecora_FinalReport.pdf.

INDEX

Index

Index

Index

Index

Index

Index

Index

Index

Index

Index

Index

Index

Index

Index

Index

swaps
  credit default swaps (CDS),
    71–74, 96, 116, 130–132
  interest rate, 85–86
synthetic collateral debt
    obligations, 96–100
systemically important financial
    institutions (SIFIs), 183, 195

Tannin, Matt, 113
tax avoidance, 149–156, 160, 187–188
  Double Irish sandwich, 188
  Dutch Sandwich, 189
  Pecora report and, 178–179
  Single Malt, 189
tax evasion, 6, 157, 159, 167–168,
    187–188
taxation, 148, 150–152, 168
teaser rates, 68
temporary disequilibria, 25
terrorists, 195
Thain, John, 60
The Theory of the Leisure Class
    (Veblen), 20
too-big-to-fail (TBTF), 74, 108, 121,
    139–147
  asset management sector
    institutions, 147
  bailouts, 140–141
  implicit insurance for, 148
  subsidies, 140–145
too big to jail, 145
toxic debt, 114, 127–128
trade
  intra-firm, 150
  in property rights, 47
Treasury bonds (T-bonds), 65
Tugwell, Rexford G., 13

UBS, 6, 129, 189
UK Finance, 106
unauthorized accounts created for
    customers by Wells Fargo,
    103, 183
underwriting, 37
UniCredit, 139
upside instruments, 87
US Steel Trust, 50, 64
utility-maximizing agents, 22,
    25, 28

Varley, John, 123
Veblen, Thorstein, 11–13, 20, 23,
    27–31, 37–38, 41, 78, 190
  absentee owners, managers,
    and engineers, 28–29
  theory of sabotage, 11–12, 20,
    27, 34, 59, 76
virtual currency. *See also*
    cryptocurrencies
  bitcoin, 77, 160, 165–168
  Libra (Facebook), 160
  Litecoin, 166
  mavro, 158
Volcker, Paul, 22, 66
Volcker's paradox, 22

Wachovia, 144
Wall Street (film), 63
Ward, Keith, 26
Washington Mutual, 144
wealth
  contracts and, 47–48
  creation, 42
  disappearance from market in
    2007–2009 financial crisis, 59
  financialized

259

Index

ANASTASIA NESVETAILOVA is professor of international political economy at City, University of London, where she also directs City Political Economy Research Centre (CITY-PERC). Her main research focuses on the structure of the global financial system and processes of financialization, financial crises and governance. Her publications include *Financial Alchemy in Crisis: The Great Liquidity Illusion* (2010) and *Shadow Banking Scope, Origins Theories* (2017). She is based in London.

RONEN PALAN is an Israeli-born economist and professor of international political economy at City, University of London. His work focuses on offshore financial centers and tax havens. He is the author or editor of a number of books, including *The Imagined Economies of Globalisation* (with Angus Cameron, Sage, 2004) and *Tax Havens: How Globalization Really Works* (with Richard Murphy and Christian Chavagneux, Cornell University Press, 2010). He is based in London.

PublicAffairs is a publishing house founded in 1997. It is a tribute to the standards, values, and flair of three persons who have served as mentors to countless reporters, writers, editors, and book people of all kinds, including me.

I. F. STONE, proprietor of *I. F. Stone's Weekly*, combined a commitment to the First Amendment with entrepreneurial zeal and reporting skill and became one of the great independent journalists in American history. At the age of eighty, Izzy published *The Trial of Socrates*, which was a national bestseller. He wrote the book after he taught himself ancient Greek.

BENJAMIN C. BRADLEE was for nearly thirty years the charismatic editorial leader of *The Washington Post*. It was Ben who gave the *Post* the range and courage to pursue such historic issues as Watergate. He supported his reporters with a tenacity that made them fearless and it is no accident that so many became authors of influential, best-selling books.

ROBERT L. BERNSTEIN, the chief executive of Random House for more than a quarter century, guided one of the nation's premier publishing houses. Bob was personally responsible for many books of political dissent and argument that challenged tyranny around the globe. He is also the founder and longtime chair of Human Rights Watch, one of the most respected human rights organizations in the world.

• • •

For fifty years, the banner of Public Affairs Press was carried by its owner Morris B. Schnapper, who published Gandhi, Nasser, Toynbee, Truman, and about 1,500 other authors. In 1983, Schnapper was described by *The Washington Post* as "a redoubtable gadfly." His legacy will endure in the books to come.

Peter Osnos, *Founder*